Parenting Children with ADHD

Successful Parenting Strategies to Handle and Calm Down a Hyperactive Child

Amber Perry

Table of Contents

Introduction

C hildren with attention deficit hyperactivity disorder (ADHD) cannot process information as easily as those without it. However, the reason this happens is still unknown.

Researchers became interested in discovering why children with attention deficit hyperactivity disorder showed differences in their brains' chemistry compared to those without the disease. These are referred to as chemical differences. To verify their theory, they administered traditional ADHD drugs to them, regulating their thinking and concentration.

After observation, the researchers concluded that children with attention deficit hyperactivity disorder had a more active dopamine transporter.

First, if you have a child with ADHD, you must learn about ADHD, its possible causes, and how you can help your child deal with the disorder's symptoms. ADHD can cause many difficulties in children and adolescents, but there are many things you can do to help.

Do not be afraid to talk and ask your child's doctor or school about any concerns you may have.

Second, do not let your feelings, emotions, or reactions hinder the healing process. Managing your response to your child with ADHD is important. If you give in to your frustration, you only harm your child and yourself.

Third, you can help your child get the medical diagnosis he/she needs to start learning to manage this disorder. That is important as it is required to access the appropriate treatment, including medication. Family doctors or pediatricians can begin the long process of diagnosis.

Fourth, do what you can as a parent. That means if they are watching television, you watch with them, not just in the room. If they are listening to music, put in an earphone and participate. Even cook food together.

Counselors are trained to help parents deal with the mental stress of raising a child with ADHD. They can give you the skills to teach your child to curb the effects of ADHD and help you build a stronger relationship with your child.

Although there is an ongoing debate between psychologists and psychiatrists on the true cause of ADHD, it has been established that it is a biological disorder. It is classified as brain impairment, and even though there are genetic factors that come into play, there is no single established gene that causes ADHD.

In children, those with classic ADHD are typically diagnosed after age five. If either you or your spouse has ADHD, there is a 50% chance that your children will also have this condition. ADHD can also be hereditary, meaning if one parent has it, their children are more likely to have it.

On the other hand, environmental factors, like diet, drugs, alcohol, tobacco, television, and limited time spent with parents, can also contribute to the development of ADHD, but only as small factors. For example, research has shown that the less exposure a child has to cigarettes in their daily life, the less likely they will be diagnosed with the condition.

It is a rare genetic disorder that leads to a deficiency in neurotransmitters, the chemicals in the brain that carry messages between cells.

It is no surprise that children with ADHD can develop behavioral and emotional problems from constant frustration. These factors include genetics, diet, limited parental care, early childhood problems, brain injuries or infections, and family environment.

In ADHD children, the brain's action takes longer to respond and respond with muddy and unclear expectations. We know this as the brain "forgets" information faster than it should.

Children with ADHD exhibit several common behaviors, including:

- Hyperactivity
- Easily distracted
- Impulsivity
- Inattentive nature
- Boredom
- Inability to focus
- Restless
- Speak quickly in noisy voices
- Learning difficulties
- Uncoordinated
- Lose things
- Poor handwriting
- Tantrums
- Hitting or biting
- Creating challenges for themselves and their families

Some children will have many of these symptoms, impairing their social and school life. These children are at high risk of dropping out of school later in life and have a low employment rate.

The diagnosis of ADHD is not easy. Other conditions have similar symptoms but are not as severe. ADHD is a neuro-behavioral disorder, and some signs are far more than normal behavior. These children often have extreme and odd behavior and social and school-life impairments. The symptoms are learned behavior and how the mind has been wired through the years.

Chapter 1:
Understanding ADHD

A lmost all teens suffer outbursts of uncontrollable behavior. They may go at a breakneck pace, make incessant noise, refuse to wait their turn, and collide with everything in their path. They may also wander off as though daydreaming, unable to concentrate or complete activities.

Although these outbursts are a passing phase for many teens, for some, they are indicative of greater concerns. Teens with ADHD, for example, frequently have difficulties interacting with siblings and other teens at school, home, and other places. Those who have difficulty paying attention struggle to learn. In addition, their impetuous tendency may put them at risk physically. As a result of their difficulty moderating their behavior, teens with ADHD may be labeled "bad teens" or "space cadets."

There is an effective therapy. If your child has ADHD, your pediatrician can prescribe a long-term treatment plan to help them live a happy and healthy life. You play a critical part in this treatment as a parent.

Left untreated, ADHD can lead to life-long issues such as poor academic performance, run-ins with the police, unsuccessful relationships, and the inability to hold a job.

The Buildup of ADHD

Unsurprisingly, ADHD is believed to be inherited. Children have temperamental variances from birth and differ from one another from birth to pre-adolescence. The challenges that an ADHD child faces in infancy, for example, are most likely due to those temperamental genetic variances.

Furthermore, it is well-known that certain temperaments tend to run in families. Some families have high-strung children, while others have calmer youngsters. There is no such thing as an all-or-nothing temperamental trait. It's akin to being tall. There are many heights, from the extremely short to the very tall. However, it may be difficult to be 4' 6" or 7' 2"; most people, short or tall, do not have an illness.

Similarly, most high-strung behaviors aren't harmful unless they're extreme. The characteristics we've covered concerning ADHD youngsters are present in all children. However, they are present in youngsters with ADHD to a significant degree, and these children have an excess of and a deficiency of some typical qualities.

Some parents typically experience similar issues when their child is of age, which might give helpful information for assisting the teen. When parents downplay the challenges caused by ADHD, the awareness can be damaging.

Suppose the parents are hesitant to admit (even to themselves) that ADHD has caused (or continues to cause) them issues. In that case, the parents may minimize their child's problems. However, if this occurs, the parents may overlook major concerns with their child that require attention.

Many teens with ADHD struggle in school because they are easily distracted and have poor attention spans. Grades may suffer due to the teen's lack of ADHD therapy.

These teens often forget homework, misplace textbooks, and are bored with everyday classwork. They may be inattentive or overly attentive and may not wait their turn before responding. They might talk over their teacher and students and speed through homework.

Common Signs and Symptoms of ADHD

It's common for teens to struggle with attention and to behave at some point in their lives. Likewise, teens with ADHD do not just outgrow their issues. Instead, the symptoms persist, are often severe, and cause problems at school, at home, or with friends.

Easy distractibility or a short attention span are two characteristics of ADHD teens virtually always present. This issue is less evident than hyperactivity, but it is more practical. A stick-to-it attitude is one that few with ADHD have. Compared to adults, young teens have a limited capacity to concentrate and complete long and arduous tasks. They may also:

- Daydream
- Frequently forget or misplace items
- Can't avoid temptation
- Struggle to take turns

During testing, a psychologist may notice that the child is paying attention. A physician may see that the child was not distracted during the quick office examination. They are all accurate, but what matters is how the child responds when an adult tries to convince the child to pay attention. Many ADHD teens can pay attention for a short period. Suppose the examiner, child psychiatrist, physician, or psychologist is unaware of the possible fluctuation of such behavior. In that case, they may wrongly conclude that the child is OK and that the parents or teacher are reacting excessively.

The capacity to persist with a specific task for an extended period may mask the distractibility in certain ADHD teens. It is usually an activity that teens pick themselves. It is sometimes socially beneficial (e.g., reading), and other times it is not. The child may appear "locked on" and indestructible, or they may be persistent. Furthermore, the action can be repeated for an extended period. Such perplexing activity in an obviously distractible child may perplex a parent, who may wonder how their child can focus so deeply on a video games but won't do homework. They are likely disappointed to hear that it is common for children who c suffer from ADHD.

Many other problems may have similar symptoms, such as anxiety, depression, difficultly sleeping, and learning challenges. One element of the approach to rule out other conditions with symptoms comparable to ADHD is a medical assessment, which includes hearing and vision tests.

Children as young as three years old are prone to hyperactivity. With or without therapy, the hyperactive symptoms usually fade away with time as children who do not have ADHD will learn to think before acting.

However, because of ADHD, some teens' continue to act without thinking. Problems paying attention may only be noticeable when school responsibilities grow. Unfortunately, these issues frequently persist until adolescence and adulthood. People with these issues might benefit from routines, study skills, and coping mechanisms.

There are no ADHD tests available. Your child's pediatrician may make a diagnosis. To make a diagnosis, doctors need information from both home and school. So, they question the parents and the child and examine the child to ensure that there are no medical issues.

Doctors frequently urge parents and teachers to report any unusual behaviors they have observed. Some doctors use the "Vanderbilt" form, while others use the "Conners" version. These are similar forms. The data that parents and instructors provide on these forms is useful.

Every child has difficulty paying attention at times. Every child is hyperactive or acts without thinking at times. However, when school-aged teens act in this manner frequently or consistently, it can generate issues at home and school.

- **Learning Disabilities:** Up to 30% of teens with ADHD have learning difficulties. Reading, writing, spelling, and math issues may result.
- **Conduct Disorder:** Teens with ADHD and ODD are more likely to acquire conduct disorder, a more extreme antisocial

behavior style. These teens are prone to lying and stealing. Others are bullied or fight. They are more vulnerable to substance misuse as teenagers. They require emergency assistance.

- **Anxiety and Depression:** Approximately 25% of teens with ADHD are also nervous or depressed. These issues are treatable, and ADHD treatment may assist in resolving these issues. Similarly, treating anxiety or sadness may aid in the improvement of ADHD.
- **Oppositional Defiant Disorder (ODD):** This condition affects as many as 33% of teens with ADHD. These are rebellious and obstinate teens.
- **Tic Disorders:** Eye blinks or facial twitches are common in teens with tic disorders. They may regularly clear their throats, snort, sniff, or yell out words. They have no control over their actions. Tourette's condition is the most severe kind of tics. This condition affects just a small percentage of teens.

The evaluation method determines whether the issue is caused by something other than ADHD.

Types of ADHD

Based on the key symptoms involved, experts have recognized three forms of ADHD:

- Inattention
- Hyperactivity and impulsivity
- A blend of inattention and hyperactivity

Inattentiveness

ADD was first used to characterize the inattentive form of ADHD. When someone experienced consistent signs of inattention and distractibility, but few indicators of hyperactivity or impulsivity, a medical or mental health professional would have diagnosed ADD.

They'd most probably diagnose ADHD now if inattention were the primary symptom.

The most common symptoms of inattentive ADHD are:

- Easily distracted
- Frequent forgetfulness in everyday life
- Difficulty paying attention to the details or listening when others speak
- Trouble focusing on tasks or activities
- Difficulty following instructions and completing tasks as directed
- A propensity to lose focus or get tripped up easily
- Difficulty staying organized or managing time
- A propensity to put off assignments that need long periods of mental effort

These indicators might appear in schools, work, home, or personal relations.

With this type of ADHD, you (or your child) may:

- Struggle to keep track of special dates such as birthdays and anniversaries, and due dates for work assignments and bill payments
- Make excuses on schoolwork, chores, or even projects you adore
- Have trouble paying attention, including to things that interest you, such as the latest book in a favorite series or a friend's description of a trip

Hyperactive Type

Hyperactivity and impulsivity are hallmarks of this kind of ADHD, also known as a hyperactive-impulsive disorder. The most common symptoms of hyperactive and impulsivity ADHD are:

- Trouble sitting quietly, remaining still, or keeping in one place
- Excessive talking
- Difficulty waiting patiently or taking turns
- Frequent squirming, fidgeting, or tapping hands and feet
- Difficulty staying seated in school, work, or other situations
- Restless feelings, which may manifest as a propensity to run or climb in inappropriate situations.

These signs and symptoms will manifest themselves in a variety of ways. For instance, (or your child) may:

- Have problems waiting in long lines, traffic, or for appointments
- Jump in with their own beliefs and thoughts when others are talking
- Make rash decisions or shop impulsively
- Have emotional outbursts or find it difficult to handle strong or intense emotions

Combination Type

Inattentive and hyperactive-impulsive symptoms are seen in people with a mixed form of ADHD.

At least six signs from each category must be present in children under the age of seventeen. Adults aged 17 and above must have at least five symptoms. According to some specialists, the mixed form of ADHD is more frequent than the other two forms, particularly among adults.

Chapter 2:
Common Triggers of ADHD to Be Aware Of

Here is a list of common triggers responsible for making the symptoms of ADHD worse.

Food Additives

Some parties believe that symptoms of ADHD can be caused by food additives in food, while others disagree. There was a review done in 2012 by L. Eugene Arnold that established a link between ADHD symptoms and artificial food colorings (L. Eugene Arnold, 2012). Arnold argued that artificial food colorings are not a main cause of ADHD, but that their presence in food can make a child more prone to be diagnosed with ADHD. But the evidence was inconclusive, and thus, nothing can be said with certainty.

In the same year, another meta-analysis was done, and a similar conclusion was reached to establish a link between ADHD and artificial food colorings (Joel T. Nigg, 2012). A total of twenty-four studies were conducted under this analysis, and it said that exposure to artificial food colorings made approximately 8% of children display ADHD symptoms.

Mineral Deficiencies

Mineral deficiencies can aggravate the symptoms of ADHD, and the treatment of ADHD can cause mineral deficiencies. The medications often prescribed to minimize the impact of ADHD often suppresses the appetite. The patient eats less and misses the opportunity to replenish the needed minerals. It becomes a cycle that can spiral out of control.

However, I must say that no conclusive study in this field has proven that mineral deficiencies can cause ADHD. At the same time, lower-than-normal levels of zinc have been found in children diagnosed with ADHD. And these studies have also shown that using zinc supplements during the treatment of ADHD can help in managing the symptoms.

Stress

A person with ADHD often overreacts to nominal situations, leading to elevated stress levels. Other things that can increase stress are procrastinating about important tasks, looming deadlines, and an inability to focus. All these things make the person anxious, which is a symptom that gives rise to stress.

Unfortunately, some stress in our lives is inevitable, and we must find a middle ground. Left unmanaged, stress can exacerbate ADHD symptoms. Follow techniques that will help you cope with your emotional and cognitive stress. Maintaining proper routines also helps.

Poor Sleep

Insufficient sleep also aggravates ADHD symptoms. Stimulants are common medications used to treat ADHD, which can cause an increase in a patient's dopamine levels. This increase in dopamine levels is what assists in dealing with ADHD but it also results in poor sleep.

When they are prescribed stimulants, patients tend to sleep poorly or not at all. They may experience daytime sleepiness or lethargy resulting from poor sleep. Lack of sleep can intensify the symptoms of ADHD. It can lead to impulsivity, indecisiveness, and inattentiveness. It has also been noticed that patients often experience sleep problems when the stimulants are administered before bedtime.

Sleep is vital to a person's overall health, and a lack of it may cause problems in school and work because of an inability to understand and concentrate.

Technology

There are many controversies regarding whether technology adds to the problem of ADHD and intensify the symptoms or not. It is said that a person with ADHD will experience aggravated symptoms if they are over-exposed to cell phones, computers, or the internet. This is not to say that loud music or watching TV will lead to ADHD; however, too much TV has been shown to make it worse.

Instead of screen time, go for a walk. It will help more than sitting in front of the TV. Go out with friends for entertainment or a meal. Being away from home helps minimize the opportunity for TV, video games, or other screen-based amusement. Although there are no formal guidelines as to how much screen time is too much, discussing the matter with a physician can help determine what may work.

Chapter 3:
What to Expect When Your Child Has ADHD

Accept Your Child as He or She Is.

You cannot fight the symptoms of ADHD. As a parent of a child with ADHD, one of the most important things I learned was to let my child simply be who he was and to express the myriad of emotions and thoughts he wished to share with me. Regarding ADHD, symptoms such as hyperactivity and impulsiveness can decrease over time. Even if they don't, acceptance is vital if you and your child are to move in a positive direction. ADHD has different manifestations from age to age.

Preschool Children with ADHD

ADHD is most often diagnosed in children once they are at school, but younger children can also display clear signs of the disorder.

Currently, between 2 and 6 percent of preschoolers are thought to have ADHD—which is a smaller percentage than that found in school-aged children (11 percent). All young children are active and energetic, but preschool children with ADHD display these qualities at a much higher or more intense level. At this age, behavioral therapy is usually the chosen method, with stimulant and other treatment-based approaches only used if therapy does not work.

Common signs of ADHD in preschool-aged children include:

- Difficulty following directions
- Waiting for one's turn
- Not paying attention
- Finding it hard to stay put

Children aged four who are diagnosed with ADHD follow a small percentage of their parents' instructions. Indeed, their child's inability to follow directions at an age-appropriate level often prompts parents to seek help.

Health professionals usually ask parents (and one or more other adults who are in close contact with the child) various questions contained in dedicated screening questionnaires to make a diagnosis. It is important to find out how the child behaves in other settings (for instance, at preschool or in other people's homes) so the professional has a clear picture of the frequency and severity of their symptoms. The professional may also test for other potential conditions that can mimic ADHD—including anxiety, depression, or sleep issues.

Behavioral Programs Used with Preschool Children

The first line of treatment for preschool children is behavioral therapy, such as parental training. Some popular programs include The Incredible Years, Positive Parenting Program (Triple P), and Parent Management Training (PMT). These aim to improve positive parent-child interactions and to teach parents skills that will help reduce behavioral issues in children. The earlier children start, the better; obtaining a diagnosis when your child is in preschool provides you with an excellent opportunity to begin this type of therapy.

Studies have shown that parental training has positive results. One study found that mothers who utilized the Triple P program reported significant improvements in maternal depression and anxiety, mother-child relationships, stress, and child behavior. Many of these programs have a long history of success. The Triple P program, for instance, started more than thirty years ago and is the subject of many published papers, clinical trials, studies, and evaluations.

When is Medication Considered?

Because few studies have examined the effect of long-term use of stimulants at this age, health professionals should be cautious about prescribing them. Medication is sometimes prescribed in a select number of cases, including:

- When a child does not respond to behavioral treatment.
- When a child poses a risk of injury to themselves or others.
- When a child is asked to leave daycare or preschool.
- When the child may have had a nervous system injury (including premature birth or exposure to toxic substances)
- When a parent is on the edge of a mental breakdown because of the child's behavior.

School-Aged Children with ADHD

Children may fidget in class, daydream, interrupt the teacher or their classmates, lose their work, and find it hard to sit still. Seeking a diagnosis is important because the squirmy child may not have ADHD. Instead, that child may have a learning disorder like dyslexia and act out in class because they are frustrated. Generally, children who have ADHD display similar behaviors in various settings. The aim of parents and health professionals at this age is to ensure that the child is correctly diagnosed to provide them with the right therapy or treatment.

Generally, behavior management treatments have positive effects on child compliance, ADHD symptoms, parent-child interactions, parenting, and parenting stress. There are several recommended approaches used with children in this age group:

- Teen Triple P (used with tweens and teens)
- Incredible Years Parenting Program (designed for children aged two to twelve)
- Parent-Child Interaction Therapy (which aims to help children feel calm and good about themselves and teaches parents the skills they need to master challenging behaviors)

A doctor may also prescribe medication for a school-aged child with ADHD. The American Academy of Pediatrics recommends parental training in behavior management for children under six and a combination of medicine and behavioral training for those aged six and above (Centers for Disease Control and Prevention, n.d.). Some parents choose to try out alternative approaches—including the Monarch External Trigeminal Nerve Stimulation (eTNS) System. Children aged seven to twelve who are not on ADHD medication can use this device.

ADHD in Teens

Teens with ADHD may be easily distracted, have poor concentration and problems with their grades, and may make decisions impulsively or fidget in their seats. As with younger children, they may lose their homework, not wait their turn to speak or participate in activities, interrupt others, or complete assignments too quickly.

ADHD also poses a driving risk for teens, who are more likely to have a vehicle accident than their peers without ADHD. However, teens who drive but take their medication can significantly lower their risk of accidents. Parents can help by discussing driving privileges.

Drug and alcohol abuse is common for all teens. Parents can minimize the risk by discussing the dangers of drug and alcohol use with their children.

Moreover, ensuring their child has the right treatment can also help lower the likelihood of substance abuse.

Teens with ADHD and Relationships

Children with ADHD have a higher risk of being bullied. Although not all teens have problems with others, some are teased or ostracized if they are shy or impulsive. Parents can help their children by encouraging social interactions, giving them pointers about social expectations, and setting up social behavior goals for their children.

Programs for Teens

Some experts believe that behavior therapy is sufficient to treat ADHD in children. However, many children continue to take ADHD medication into their teens as recommended by their health team. Usually, a combination of both approaches provides positive results. Specific programs like Teen Triple T teach parents five important skills:

1. How to use assertive discipline
2. Set realistic expectations
3. Care for themselves
4. Create a positive learning environment for their children
5. Build a safe, interesting environment

Some families also try alternative treatments such as Chinese medicine, memory training, neurofeedback, and the like, often alongside medication. They rely on strategies such as setting clear rules for home, school, and social settings and establishing a routine for their teen children. They may also include other activities they excel at and enjoy (from science clubs to art, music, or any hobby that ignites a child's passion).

Modifiable Lifestyle Factors

Some lifestyle factors—including watching too much television or not enjoying good sleep quantity and quality—can exacerbate ADHD symptoms. Some believe that when children spend more time on cognitively stimulating activities in childhood, there is a reduced chance of the onset of ADHD symptoms. Just a few examples of cognitively stimulating activities include games and puzzles, word games, math problems, reading—anything and everything that challenges one's brain to think.

Situations Your Child May Thrive In

You may find that your child displays positive behaviors in some situations more than others. These include those in which they can receive immediate rewards for complying with instructions and moments in which they receive individual attention. Because children with ADHD may have trouble waiting for long term rewards, they tend to appreciate those ones that don't require too much focus. They also enjoy being alone with a parent or teacher because issues such as interruption or waiting for one's turn are not as problematic as they can be in a group setting.

Do Children Outgrow ADHD?

Most people do not outgrow ADHD, but they can learn important ways to manage it and achieve success in work and personal relationships. One survey found that about half of adults with ADHD can hold full-time jobs, compared to 72 percent of adults without the disorder. Adults with ADHD also find that some behaviors (distraction, procrastination, and inattentiveness) can trigger relationship conflicts.

People with ADHD can thrive professionally and personally with the right treatment and strategies. In personal settings, useful tips for adults and children include setting a time to talk and battling forgetfulness with reminder and time management apps. Actively avoiding hyperfocus during mealtimes can be accomplished by encouraging the hyper-focused person to get up and move around until they can be more "present."

At work, adults with ADHD can take several steps to stay focused and meet their daily tasks. These include keeping online planners or calendars, working in a quiet and uncluttered space, and scheduling time to answer text messages and emails. It may also include breaking big goals into smaller ones, setting a time for the completion of each goal, and delegating time-consuming tasks to an assistant so one can concentrate on more important goals.

Adults with ADHD should also try to find a good work-life balance, eat healthily, and reward themselves for their achievements.

Chapter 4:
How I Influence My Child's Behavior

C hildren are learning machines and must know their place in the world and adapt their behaviors to fit in those places. Therefore, to address ADHD without addressing the social dynamics surrounding a child is to do them a disservice. Our children do not live in a vacuum, so as we take a closer look at this disorder, we must put it in proper perspective.

Of all the social dynamics that a child must learn to adapt to and fit in, the family is the most important. In most cases, the future success of a child with ADHD hinges on how the family responds to their needs. Because of the close interaction with parents, siblings, and others in the household, how well the child develops can impact those missing executive skills in major ways.

For that reason, diagnosing ADHD is not as important as how the diagnosis will affect the family dynamics. A diagnosis does not determine how successful the treatment will be or how the child will overcome the challenges they face. The parents as primary caretakers will have the most impact and influence on the child's progress through the hurdles they must face with ADHD. With that in mind, every parent must ask themselves how their reaction to their child's behavior will influence their progress.

This psychological exercise will reveal your child's weaknesses and your own. It is no secret that managing a child with ADHD is not easy. Their inability to control emotions, follow through on certain tasks, or attain a certain level of independence can bring out the worst in many of us, especially busy parents.

So, ask yourself how you react when you're at your wit's end, when cajoling, negotiating, yelling, prompting, and bribing are ineffective. At this point, you must be entirely truthful with yourself because your reaction may be a contributing factor in your child's ability to adjust to this disorder.

This part is intended to give you a bird's eye view of your family dynamics and how they may affect your child. The questions asked can be hard to accept, but if you are open and honest about the answers, you will reap the rewards.

1. Are you married, or are you a single parent? If married, is your relationship positive, or do you allow the negative aspects to spill over onto your children? Do you see your spouse or partner as a source of support or the opposite?
2. Do you work outside the home? If so, is your job stressful, and do you sometimes bring that stress home with you?
3. Does your work bring you professional satisfaction, or does it drain you of your energy, leaving you unfulfilled?
4. How do the children interact with their sibling who has ADHD? How much of that interaction is monitored and regulated, and what examples have you set for the family?

It cannot be overstressed that the family dynamics of a child with ADHD are critical in understanding the child and helping them to navigate the challenges they will encounter. Not only do these interactions tend to be more stressful, but evidence has shown that these interactions can have a huge impact on a child's psychological state. Some statistics seem to indicate that since the disorder can be genetic, there is a chance that a child with ADHD also has a parent with ADHD. The problem increases exponentially for the entire family. Here is how it usually goes:

1. Parents who are already involved in personal problems see their child's behavior as an intrusion on their stressful lives. The ADHD child's disruptive tendencies are perceived as consuming their valuable time and demanding too much from them.
2. Parents react negatively to the child's conduct with harsh punishments, emotional outbursts, and irritability.

25

3. Parents may withdraw words of encouragement, recognition for good behavior, and the normal warmth and love that every child needs.
4. The child then responds in kind, usually in defiance, stubbornness, or some other negative emotion or attitude.
5. The behavior is then reinforced in the parent's mind, identifying the child as rebellious or a disruptive influence in the family.
6. The cycle then repeats.

It becomes a circle that never ends. The parents are stressed and withdraw the affections that the child needs. Then, the child responds to negative input negatively, and the cycle repeats. This cycle may repeatedly occur throughout the child's lifetime spreading to all other family members. In the end, you have a dysfunctional family unit, and no one is happy.

Many may not even realize that they are doing it, but it is up to the parents to stop the cycle and get the family on a more nurturing and positive track. Breaking the circle may be much harder if the parent involved also has ADHD.

Difference Between Mother's and Father's Interactions with ADHD

Some parents comment that there is a difference in how a child with ADHD responds to them. Often mothers point out that they tend to have more difficulty with their children than the fathers do. One study did show that children tended to give more negative responses to mothers than they did with their fathers.

While the reason for this is unclear, there are a few theories that may explain this problem within the family dynamic. One primary theory is that in most families, the mother is the primary caretaker and as she is trying to reign in the child's self-control. As a result, negative reactions tend to occur. She is more likely to engage in conflicts with the child than the father, who takes a lesser role in the managing of ADHD skills.

Mothers also tend to be more verbal in reasoning with their children than fathers do. Since children with ADHD generally struggle with language expression, are less likely to respond to verbal guidance, and less likely to absorb the instructions given and, therefore, will quickly become irritated. Conversely, fathers are not usually the ones to spend a lot of time repeating instructions and maybe quicker to punish when results are not met. Therefore, one may draw the conclusion that a parent who talks less and follows through quickly seems to be the one that the ADHD child is most likely to respond to.

Interactions Between ADHD Children and Their Siblings

Next, the dynamics of the ADHD child with his siblings must also be carefully analyzed. It is well-known that children with ADHD are more likely to argue, fight, and encourage improper behavior. Their poor behavior will inevitably create more conflicts in the household.

There is no question that it can be frustrating living with a child who has ADHD. It's no wonder that children without the disorder may feel put upon and treated unfairly. Siblings may resent their sibling because they share an additional burden of responsibility at home when they are expected to pick up the slack with chores that the ADHD child has yet to master. There may also be some envy as they notice that the child with ADHD gets more attention and help from the parents than they do.

All these factors can serve as fuel for an already tense situation and, if not handled correctly, could lead to major difficulties for everyone.

What Does it Mean?

It all leads to the simple fact that having anyone with ADHD in the home can be stressful, but it is even more stressful when it is a child. Living with ADHD impacts everyone, so treatment must also include everyone. Dealing with ADHD is challenging in the best of situations, so it's important for all involved to recognize this.

Chapter 5:
Supporting a Child with ADHD

The ADHD experience for a child and their parents is both exhilarating and frustrating. As parents, you help your child overcome challenges and teach them to channel their energy into positive activities. Doing so will enable them to fit in, work better, and connect with siblings and in school. The chances of success are considerably higher when you address ADHD earlier rather than later.

Children with ADHD usually have deficits in executive functions, which greatly affect their ability to plan, think, and control their impulses. As a result, you must take over the executive functioning for your child initially and provide extra guidance for them as they gain these skills on their own as they go through life.

You may feel that these ADHD symptoms are tiring, but remember that your child finds this exhausting and exasperating. Children with ADHD want a clean, organized space and to do what their parents ask of them, but it isn't as easy for a child with ADHD to accomplish. Positivity and support are essential for you and your child. What's more, patience and compassion are vital at this point. ADHD is manageable, and so is having a stable and happy home at the same time.

Parenting and coping with ADHD

Parents whose children have ADHD need to take care of their child by taken care of themselves. Following are a few things parents can do:

Keep positive and healthy

As a parent, you have the tools to maintain a healthy physical and emotional environment. Try to control the factors that positively impact the symptoms of ADHD that your child has. A positive attitude will set the tone for the household, and combined with common sense, can ease the stresses of managing ADHD.

Find individualized counseling

As a parent, you cannot do it all. You need professional help, whether you like it or not, because it is not only beneficial for your child but also for you. Do not be afraid to seek assistance especially when a child's behavior starts to affect your own mental needs—this happens, and it does not mean you are not a good parent. A therapist will be able to help manage your anxiety and stress as well as that of your child's. At the end of the actual day, you need support.

Keep things in perspective

Keep in mind that your child's reactions and behavior stem from the disorder from which they suffer. Often, these behaviors are not intentional. When everything threatens to overwhelm you, keep things in perspective. Maintain a sense of humor; while things may seem embarrassing and frustrating now, you'll laugh about it down the road.

Make small concessions

Don't make a big deal about it if your child left one chore undone or forgot to complete one section of their homework when they did the other three. Instead, celebrate what they did accomplish.

Believe in them

Positivity and encouragement do wonders both mentally and physically. Praise your child's good behavior so they know when they did the right thing. Your family may now fight ADHD, but it's not going to last forever. You need to believe in your child's abilities and remember that they will learn, change, discover, and grow. When things don't go as planned and frustration creeps in, always remind yourself that your child will be successful.

For the child with ADHD, parents can build a home that supports their needs. Following are some examples that are known to help children with ADHD find success in everyday tasks.

Establish structure

Predictable patterns enable children with ADHD to flourish, excel, and accomplish their tasks and chores. Instill a structured routine for your family to create stability in the home. It provides that sense of security, but your child knows what is expected of them and can prioritize their time.

Follow a routine

Set aside a specific time for chores and tasks. Outline details on what to do and how to do it to help children meet expectations. It can be as simple as brushing their teeth in the morning, having rituals for mealtimes, and setting time to do homework and playtime. Other things could be putting away toys after playtime, laying out their clothes for the next morning before bed, having TV time at a certain hour, and keeping their school supplies in a specific space at home.

Use clocks and timers

Display clocks around the house, including in your child's bedroom. Encourage them to look at the clock to gauge their next step. It doubles as a tool that helps them learn to read the time. Build in time for transitional activities, such as cleaning up after playing and doing quieter activities as bedtime gets closer.

Simplify your child's schedule

Although it may seem rigid to create schedules, they give a child with ADHD a sense of predictability in their lives. That said, it does not mean you have filled your child's day with too many activities; they may end up more distracted than they already are.

Break tasks into manageable chunks

A calendar works great for this. Use a huge one with colors and highlights to remind your child of their chores and tasks. Use color codes to track homework, chores, and playtime, so they do not feel overwhelmed with tasks and schoolwork. You can also breakdown morning routines so it can be smaller tasks.

Create a quiet place at home

A private and quiet place is essential for your child. This space can be their bedroom, a reading nook, or the porch. It is a safe and comfortable space for your child to complete homework, read, or have quiet time, but it should not be the same place they go if they are punished.

Keep your spaces organized

It can be hard to keep a home organized and tidy with children around, but endeavor to keep things in their places. Lead by example with organization and neatness so your child can follow suit.

Take breaks

Being supportive all the time is not always possible. You also might think of getting a childcare professional. Good options for breaks include:

1. Stretching
2. Patting the dog
3. Meditating

4. Minute self-care

Reduce distractions

Children with ADHD are easily distracted, so it is important to regulate things like computer time, electronic devices, TV time, and even video games that encourage impulsive behavior. Instead, do more activities outside the home so your child has a channel for built-up energy.

Encourage movement and sleep

Children with ADHD have loads of energy to burn, which is why participating in sports and other activities that require physical exertion can help them channel this energy in a conducive way. As we all know, physical activity and exercise have benefits, from improving concentration, decreasing anxiety and depression, and promoting brain growth.

As children with ADHD benefit from a night of good sleep, encouraging them to participate in something that burns that restless energy will also help them sleep. You can get your child to join a sport that suits their strengths and is something they will enjoy. Individual or team sports such as hockey and basketball are good options as they require constant motion. Yoga and martial arts are excellent physical activities as they help enhance cognitive control.

Anyone is less attentive with insufficient sleep; however, the effects are exacerbated among children with ADHD. Their attention issues often cause trouble falling asleep which is why consistent bedtime routines are essential in preventing this problem.

Promote Wait Time

This strategy can help them control their impulses to think before speaking. It teaches children how to give a momentary pause before replying or talking. You can also encourage when they do their homework by asking interactive questions on their favorite books, favorite characters, why they like a certain color, what their day was like today, and other conversational pieces so it can help your child formulate better responses.

Encourage out-loud thinking

The lack of self-control in children with ADHD causes them to act and speak without thinking. It is also imperative to understand the thought process of your child to help them curb their impulsive behaviors.

Set expectations and rules

Consistent rules are key for children with ADHD so that they can focus and follow. These rules that must be simple and clear, and placed somewhere prominent in the house so it's easy to see. Organization works best for children with ADHD, so create corresponding incentives and penalties will teach them about consequences. For children with ADHD specifically, bear in mind that they deal with a higher rate of criticism than those without. Children with ADHD are more aware of their shortcomings, so if they behave well, praise them since they often get so little of it. If they have complaints about their behavior or have done something wrong, tell them what the consequences are.

As a positive comment, a smile, a hug, or any other reward that you can give to improve concentration, attention, as well as impulse control of your child with ADHD is always good. Celebrate small achievements and good behavior. Focus on positive reinforcements when it comes to inappropriate behavior or poor performance.

A note about using rewards and consequences:

REWARDS:

Reward good behavior with activities they like, praise, and privileges instead of giving them food or toys.

Change your rewards often since children with ADHD are easily bored.

Create a chart with a star system: stars for good behavior, so there's a visual reminder for your children.

Make rewards fast and immediate rather than giving a promise in the future, though small rewards that work to bigger ones also work.

CONSEQUENCES:

All consequences need to be spelled out beforehand; follow through if your child misbehaves.

Time-outs and removing privileges are one of the ways of administering consequences.

You can also remove your child from environments and situations that could trigger misbehavior.

If the child misbehaves, ask them what can be done differently. You can also demonstrate.

Always follow through with a consequence.

Practice Better Eating Habits

Remember that diet is not a specific ADHD trigger. However, certain foods, especially those with additives, can affect a child's mental state, impacting their behavior. Monitor what your child consumes, especially when eating out and in school. What they eat, how much, and when they eat can reduce the symptoms of ADHD.

Choose fresh rather than processed foods, adhere to regular mealtimes, and eliminate junk food. Poor dietary habits become more prevalent among children with ADHD. They are prone to distraction and impulsivity, leading to overeating, undereating, disordered eating, and missed meals. Forgetfulness, especially involving meals, is a common concern in a child with ADHD. They can go without food for hours and will binge on whatever foodstuff they find. The result is a devastating pattern of eating, which affects the growing child's physical and emotional health.

Creating a schedule involving regular mealtimes and a nutritious menu with an allocated snack time can prevent unhealthy eating habits. A child with ADHD physically needs regular healthy food intake. Mentally, mealtimes are necessary as it provides schedule rhythm and a break from their tasks.

Dietary reminders:

- Remove junk food from home and pantry
- Sugary foods are off-limits when dining out
- No TV during mealtimes
- Provide vitamin and mineral supplements

Help your Child Improve their Social Skills

Simple social interactions prove to be another hurdle for children with ADHD. They struggle with talking too much, often cannot read social cues, interrupt frequently, or appear too intense or aggressive. Because they mature differently from their peers, children with ADHD can be a subject of teasing and bullying. Despite their emotional immaturity, children with ADHD are gifted with an acute sense of creativity and intelligence. Often, they figure out ways to cope with their situation and exist harmoniously with other children when they can't be friends. Their personality traits can sometimes exasperate parents and teachers, but they may be considered funny and charming to their peers.

Social skills and rules can be a hurdle for children with ADHD. In this area, you can help them become better listeners or even become better at reading people's faces and body language when they interact with their peers:

- Show them how to change their behavior by speaking gently and honestly with them about their challenges.
- Help your child through various scenarios by doing some role-play to make learning social skills fun. Choose playmates who have similar abilities and language capacities as your child, so they do not feel out of place.
- At first, invite only one or two friends. Pay attention while they are playing and have a policy of zero tolerance for hitting, pushing, and screaming.

Teaching Students with ADHD

Children with ADHD can do very well in school, especially if the child's teacher works with parents to devise a routine that fits the classroom and is similar in structure to the home. However, parents and teachers must work together; neither can be successful without the other.

Teachers play a vital role in the student's life, and when ADHD strategies are employed in a classroom setting, this can demonstrate to the child that they are worthwhile and capable. The child will believe this, and positive results will follow through.

There are some strategies a teacher can employ that are especially helpful for students with ADHD but benefit all the students in a classroom. That structure is a safety net that helps students focus on their work and establishes an inclusive and supportive classroom, encourages learning, enforces discipline, and boosts self-esteem.

Make rules and routines

It is just not at home that rules and routines are important. Requirements for students with and without ADHD. Set short, simple rules in the classroom and a system for feedback.

Provide positive feedback

Positive reinforcement and feedback are essential. Instead of saying NO, you cannot do this, or NO you cannot do that, give students an outlet or a template of what is expected of them. You can say, "When you get into class, check the board for your assignments before you do anything else," or, "When you enter class, speak when you have settled in your desk." Your instructions could also be, "Find your seats first, and then you may talk quietly with your friend. When I start teaching, the conversations need to stop."

Establish classroom structure

Structure helps all students in the classroom and is especially beneficial for students with ADHD. Students are better able to stay on task as the distractions are minimum. Some of these routines include having row or table captains who collect assignments at the end of the day. You can also make it a point for ADHD students to check in with the teacher, a peer, or row captain to see if the assignment is understood and if there's anything they may need to clarify.

Give appropriate supervision to ADHD students.

Remember that all students need appropriate supervision. Ensure that teachers give your child the supervision necessary to provide a safe learning environment.

Chapter 6:
Reducing Conflicts with Your Child

You may notice that your child is easily distracted, talks excessively, and becomes irritable when things do not go their way if they have ADHD.

Ways to Help Reduce Conflicts by Changing How You Interact with Your Child

Use clear, direct communication

Avoid saying "NO" or "thank you." These imply you'll punish them if they don't do what you ask. Instead, tell your child what you want from them in a declarative sentence. For example, say, "I need you to sit down and finish your dinner," or, "I love having nachos for dinner." This kind of language helps children understand what you intend and why.

Minimize how often you raise your voice

Recognizing that sometimes it's inappropriate to raise your voice (in front of other people) and minimizing how often you raise your voice are important. For example, you may find it helpful to tell your child, "We're going to have a conversation about this when we are alone." Your child understands that their actions were inappropriate but that there will be an opportunity to respond when you are both calm and ready to listen.

Avoid power struggles with your child.

Children who have ADHD may have a hard time understanding what is expected. Explain the rules clearly and give plenty of reminders to help them know what's expected. Doing this in an organized manner that avoids power struggles is important for their well-being. Parents with ADHD may also find it helpful to give their children a star or other reward for following rules when possible—as an extra motivator for things like homework, chores, or reading books.

Be careful when taking away privileges.

Children with ADHD may be more sensitive to changes in routine, schedules, and privileges. For example, instead of saying, "You didn't brush your teeth tonight, so you cannot have dessert," say, "You need to brush your teeth in the morning, or you will not get dessert." With this approach, children feel more in control of their situation, and losing their favorite dessert doesn't seem too harsh.

Don't laugh at your child's behavior.

Laughing at behavior can make your child feel like they are being teased and may not take it seriously. Even if you find the behavior funny, you might say, "That was funny!" or "I love the idea of doing that with you!" instead. These kinds of responses helps redirect their attention to a new activity rather than laughing at what they did. Avoid saying phrases like "What's wrong with you?" or "Why can't you behave?" These imply something is wrong with them and leads them to believe that their ADHD is the cause of their struggles.

Separate ADHD from a character flaw.

It is easier to relate to your child when you focus on their good qualities and the work they do that you appreciate. Your child may be more accepting if you focus on those things instead of their ADHD behaviors. Asking them what they like about themselves and helping them stay positive about themselves can be beneficial.

Avoid letting anger or frustration drive your words and actions.

Consider setting time aside with your child each day to chat about the things that bother them (such as having trouble concentrating or getting back up after falling) or that they are proud of (such as doing something they are not comfortable with). This time gives you an opportunity to talk things out and give your child a safe space to express their feelings.

Avoid thinking you know what is best for your child.

Instead of saying, "You need to get back up and try again," say, "You will hurt yourself if you fall." They know that it is not their fault, but they can still learn from the experience so it doesn't happen again, of which they can be proud.

How to Deal with Unavoidable Conflict

When you have an unavoidable conflict with your child, trying not to think about the situation and seek out things you can do together can be helpful. Focusing on what you both like about each other or find fun (such as a game or activity) makes you less likely to have conflict. Try not to let the frustrations from the incident build up. Let time pass so you have time to cool down.

Take a break.

Take a walk, a bath, or do something else that relaxes you. Avoid letting the stress of the conflict build up over time. You will be able to think more clearly, concentrating on the problem and identifying solutions.

Don't make it about the child.

Don't go into a difficult situation with your child thinking about their behavior. Focus on what changes need to be made instead. This focus prevents a power struggle that becomes an opportunity for them to take advantage of you or others in your life. If your child is acting up, focus on how you would like them to feel and learn from the experience (so they are more likely to make improvements).

Seek solutions other than discipline or punishment.

You might try using "time-in" or "time-out" to help your child learn about responsibility but being creative in using these is important. For example, you could have a "time-in" for every problem they're having with schoolwork and a "time-out" for being disruptive in class. You could set more effective goals than traditional punishments (such as getting them to complete their homework) or rewards (such as suggesting they finish their homework).

In some situations, it can be helpful not to make any changes until after the conflict has passed, particularly if you worry that your child won't do it anyway. Your child will have time to think about the situation and develop a plan independently.

Consider going to a counselor.

It might be helpful to go to a counselor to better understand how ADHD works, its effect on your life, and what strategies might help in the future. With a counselor's help, you can ensure you are taking care of yourself while also helping your child reach their potential (without fighting as much) positively.

Make the change yourself.

If changing what you're doing isn't an option, try eliminating the challenges in your life that might be causing your child to have conflicts (e.g., going to bed earlier or cutting back on work hours). If needed, set up boundaries with others to help you remember this (such as putting your phone away when it's time for dinner), and consider setting limits for yourself regarding how long and how much work you need to do each day. The more control you have over how many things are happening at once, the easier it will be for you and your child to function properly in their lives.

ADHD can make it hard for your child to deal with daily tasks and responsibilities, but there are many things you can do to help prevent conflict.

Chapter 7:
Importance of ADHD

A s a parent, you have an opportunity to learn more about your child and become better equipped to handle the problems that arise. ADHD can be viewed as an asset that can benefit many people, including children and adults.

Pure Energy

In some situations, hyperactivity can be a real problem. But when you consider that it can be a blessing and use your child's energy to help him learn or accomplish something they want to do, they gain control over their ADHD. A child who can focus and concentrate and finish what they start will always be more productive in the long run.

Intense Focus

As your child becomes more responsible, they can learn to direct their ADHD energy, leading them to accomplish a specific goal, like finishing their homework by seven o'clock. So instead of being frustrated with the lack of focus in your child, help them channel this attribute into an area that will produce positive results.

Creativity and Curiosity

Children with ADHD are often inventive and imaginative. They establish new approaches to problems that others overlook or avoid altogether. This natural curiosity is productive if they harness it in the service of a worthy cause—something you might have to help them do until they learn how to accomplish this independently.

Impatience and Frustration

Sometimes, they may be impatient to learn or complete a task because they need help understanding the process or are frustrated. You can channel their frustration into productive behavior, knowing that everyone becomes frustrated at times.

Lack of Self-Discipline and Impulsiveness

An impulsive personality often accompanies ADHD symptoms and seems part of the package. Your child may be quick to act, but this impulsiveness can be a real gift in some situations. It can get them out of a dangerous situation or protect others.

Sensitivity to Others' Needs

Children with ADHD are often sensitive to others' needs and feelings—to the point that they recognize others' emotions and moods. This sensitivity helps them understand what other people need, so if you and your child learn how to channel it, they may be a natural for careers where empathy is required—teaching, social work, and health care, to name a few.

Empathy

ADHD children may not process the wide range of feelings that others experience. But they show an incredible range of empathy and pick up on emotions, even while they are overwhelmed by their own. Your child may be a natural counselor and healer if he learns how to apply this attribute productively.

Patience and Flexibility for Change

ADHD children may have difficulty understanding what others expect because their minds move quickly from one thought or idea to another. Your child often has the potential for great accomplishment but falls short because they have need help following through with one plan or project when something else is vying for their attention. Some adjustments and a little help from you can help your child become more patient and flexible.

Fearlessness

Anxiety is not usually associated with ADHD children; they enjoy life and don't worry about the future. This quality can be a great gift in the face of danger when others might freeze or run away. Your child may enjoy greater safety in dangerous situations, but you need to teach them how to take care of themself so that they don't become victims of their impulsive behavior or lack of fear.

Risk-Taking

Your child may have little or no fear of danger, but you should teach him how to know and evaluate risk before he is put in a dangerous situation. An impulsive approach can get them hurt or put them in immediate danger. But if your child learns how to control it, it can be an asset to people in the workplace or other situations where fear is not an asset.

Emotional Upset

When children have ADHD, they often feel intense emotions without processing or dealing with them effectively. They are acutely aware of others' emotions and become enraged when others do not exhibit the same emotional responses as they do. Fortunately, your child can learn to control her feelings and productively use them.

Introversion and Independence

Impulsiveness and anxiety can become real problems because they can lead to an intense desire for independence, which often involves breaking the rules for curiosity's sake. Along with that comes the need for privacy, which can be a real challenge when you have many friends and family members around all the time. You should help your child learn to be more independent while still feeling close to others through conversation.

Stimulation

All children need stimulation and entertainment to learn and stay focused. Without it, they can become bored easily or distracted by other things. Your child will seek toys, books, television, or audio sources that produce interesting sights or sounds.

Fear of Entrapment

Your child may be desperate to avoid unnecessary commitment due to their desire for freedom and independence. Yet they may find themselves trapped in the very situation they sought to avoid because they lacked the knowledge necessary to exit gracefully.

Mood Swings

You may see sudden behavioral changes when your child becomes excited about something or not getting the stimulation they need. When that happens, you can help them manage their mood swings by providing the novelty they crave, while with new things to do and new learning experiences so that their energy is not focused on unproductive excitement or boredom.

Extreme Optimism

Children with ADHD often have an enhanced sense of their abilities and can reach beyond the limits set by others because they don't comprehend those limitations. They may have an unrealistic sense of time and even their mortality. Your child may be incredibly able to see things from a positive point of view or get through difficult or boring situations. But they can also be too optimistic, which can lead to trouble since they are often unprepared for the realities of the situations they find themselves in.

Feelings of Insecurity

Your child may be able to overcome his insecurity in the face of failure, but he will still feel it and need your support. If you can help your child accept that he has limitations just like everyone else and find ways to work around them, he can avoid the sense of failure while feeling confident enough to try new things.

Physical Energy

While the restless physical energy characteristic of children with ADHD may appear to be a distraction to others, it can also be a tremendous source of productivity. If your child has the freedom to move and exercise, they will be more productive and focused overall. You need to help your child use this energy productively to avoid trouble for themselves or others.

Physical Flexibility

Physical movements may seem awkward or clumsy to others because children with ADHD have difficulty following patterns or rules of movement. But their physical flexibility makes them good at everything from drawing and writing to rocking or rolling (think of runners and divers) because they have such a wide range of movement.

Problem-Solving Abilities

While your child may need help sitting still and focusing, this does not rule out the possibility of them thinking on their feet and solving problems when necessary. This ability can be an asset to your child because it helps them overcome setbacks quickly and stay quick on their feet.

Taking advantage of your ADHD child's unique qualities can be a real challenge. Once you help your child understand that their unique qualities are an asset instead of a hindrance, you can teach them how to see the benefits in every situation and achieve more. The key to raising a child with ADHD isn't just about helping them manage their behavior. It's also about raising your child to succeed by assisting them to act on their natural strengths and skills.

Opportunities for Children with ADHD

Physical Fitness

ADHD children are adventurous and like to move around a lot. They are also physically fit, which means they have an advantage in nearly every sport or physical activity. They can push their bodies to extremes because they don't easily feel pain or exhaustion. That is why exercise is so important for your child's ADHD management; it will help them stay focused on the task at hand while also allowing them to develop a body capable of handling any physical activity.

Artistic Abilities

Many children with ADHD have artistic abilities that seem out of place in everyday life. However, that makes it a perfect fit for them, and they should use their creative talent to channel their ADHD symptoms into art instead of acting out in other ways. Artistic expression is a superb outlet for the ideas and imagination common in children with ADHD, and they can express themselves while staying focused on the task at hand.

Extraordinary Listeners

Because they have difficulty focusing on a single thing, children with ADHD often love to talk but are not good listeners. However, they can listen well when listening offers a break from other distractions. Give your child headphones; they will focus better and increase the likelihood of completing assignments while listening better and reducing distractions from outside sources.

Compulsive Cleaning and Organization

Children with ADHD often struggle to stay focused on tasks that require organization, but their compulsive need to clean and organize can be an asset. With this tendency, they can create order around the chaos of their mental world instead of letting it disrupt the rest of their lives. A messy room doesn't have to mean it is unorganized, but an organized space shows that your child has organized all the important tasks in each area of life into a place where they can easily find them when needed.

Emotional Outbursts

For children with ADHD, emotions can run high and explode without warning. They are more sensitive to outward signs of anger and fear than others. This characteristic will sometimes serve them well, but it can also be used against them if they aren't taught to control their emotions and how they express them. Many parents will punish their child for throwing a tantrum or being overcome by emotion since it is perceived as weakness, whereas controlling your emotions makes you stronger.

Insatiability

Many children with ADHD need to learn and explore new things. They are passionate about everything they do, which can be a problem in school if they don't keep a strict routine. But this trait helps them stay motivated to learn and can be seen as an asset if they are pushed to grow academically or professionally out of their comfort zone.

Quick Recovery

Because children with ADHD have trouble concentrating on a single thing, they are often seen as scatterbrained instead of enjoying the benefits of their quick responses and recovery time. They bounce back quickly from mistakes because they don't dwell on what happened or become embarrassed. They pick up the pieces and try again until they succeed or give up.

Benefits of ADHD

Low Frustration Threshold

Children with ADHD often have a low frustration threshold, which means they get bored more easily and give up early on difficult tasks. While this can be seen as a disadvantage, it's an advantage when learning new skills or trying something new. If your child never gets frustrated or stuck in a rut, they will always feel inspired to try something new, and they will be motivated to keep trying as long as necessary until they get it right. You can teach your child to channel their boredom and frustration toward positive activities, like learning how to play the piano or prepare a healthy snack.

Learn New Skills Quickly

Children with ADHD find learning new things with repetition much easier than learning through traditional instruction methods. Because they are quickly bored, they find it much easier to learn something by doing the task themselves rather than asking someone else to show them how. This skill can be used in everyday life and school if your child can learn it. Many adults with ADHD still struggle with this because they rely on others to guide them instead of doing the work themselves.

Long-Term Memory

People with ADHD may struggle to remember what they just learned, but if you give them some time to focus on the task, their knowledge and ability to retain information improve considerably. They learn faster as children and adults and can often reverse-engineer situations when trying to complete similar tasks in the future.

Quick Studies

Because they have a hard time learning from a book or teacher, they often turn to other sources for information that interest them. They can apply what they've learned from one activity to another later, making learning new skills easier because they've already "done" something similar. For example, if your child learns to draw by watching someone else draw a face step by step, they can skip the instructions and use what they've seen in their memory next time you ask them to draw you a picture of Mickey.

Finds Ways to Fix Problems

Children with ADHD may appear helpless when they find themselves stuck, but they can figure out how to fix the problem if directed. Ask them how to fix it instead of making them wait until someone else fixes it. They will tell you what they need to fix the issue on their own, and they will often surprise you with their ingenuity.

Greater Empathy for Others with the Same Disorder

Children with ADHD see the world from an energetic point of view that others may not always understand or appreciate. As children grow, they learn to manage their energetic ways, but it's often difficult to teach them how to be more restrained in social settings. If you have a child with ADHD who struggles with controlling their emotions and showing empathy in social settings, encourage them as much as possible to practice these traits in between getting annoyed from having to interact nonstop.

Strong Work Ethic

Many professionals in the workforce must be high-energy and persistent to succeed. While this can be a challenge for people with ADHD, it's an asset because it motivates them to do their best and gets them to complete their job quickly.

Learn to Negotiate Instead of Fighting

Because children with ADHD have a hard time focusing on a single thing, they often have trouble saying "no" and making decisions for themselves. Suppose something comes up that interferes with their other plans or goals. In that case, they often try to negotiate for things like getting extra time, so it won't affect their plans too much, opting out of a class if they aren't behind on work, or asking someone else to help them complete the task instead of fighting the problem head-on.

Create and Solve Problems

Many children with ADHD are creative thinkers, which means they look at situations from a much different perspective than their peers. They don't get bored following the rules and learn to use strategy when solving problems. Once they reach adulthood, you can encourage them to use those skills in the workforce by asking them to help solve a problem at work or devise a new idea for something they'd like to try.

Use Chaos as a Learning Tool

Children with ADHD often have seemingly disorganized bedrooms and living spaces. However, messiness can be the best way for your child to learn how to organize their belongings and make things flow more smoothly. Many people with ADHD work hard at organizing their homes when they grow up because they remember how frustrating disorder was when they were younger. As adults, they use the lessons they learned as children to avoid the same issues.

Children with ADHD may seem like a handful at times, but their experiences are valuable situations to help them learn how cope with their ADHD and use it for success.

Chapter 8:
Love and Compassion for Your Child with ADHD

O ften, your child quickly sets off an angry reaction in you. As a parent, you believe it is your job to demand that your child stop misbehaving. The emotional outbursts and impulsivity must be brought in line. They are unacceptable. The fact that the child continues with behaviors you has repeatedly asked him to stop feels like defiance and you do not feel affectionate during these moments. You are mad because your child appears to refuse to do what you have repeatedly told him he must do.

But now, the professionals have diagnosed your child with ADHD. They have told you this means your child cannot help doing what he does. They have said this is behavior beyond your child's control. That means what you are expecting when you discipline your child for these behaviors is unreasonable. Would that be possible?

You are working through a treatment plan in collaboration with a team of professionals, or you may be in the process of developing such a plan. You may have advice on how to create a structured home environment and how to handle discipline. Love is the most significant contribution you can deliver to your child.

Of course, you love your child, but their emotional outbursts and unpredictable mood swings seem to make showing love impossible. Your temper flares and you snap in anger at your out-of-control six-year-old when he races into the room shouting and breaks an expensive lamp. You never know what your emotionally volatile child will do at any given moment.

As a parent, you might be skeptical. You might think an ADHD child can correct behavior you dislike at will, so you punish your child for unruly behavior. But ask yourself some questions. Would you punish a blind child because you believe they can correct their vision at will? Would you punish a child with leukemia for failing to reduce the swelling of their lymph nodes by sheer will? Children with ADHD cannot control the symptoms of their disorder through willpower. Punishing symptoms cannot alter that fact.

If you have tried to manage your ADHD child this way or had ideas along these lines, you are not alone. Most parents of ADHD children have made this mistake. Like any child, your child needs to feel understood and loved. Because you are the parent, you hold a special place of importance in your child's life. The child may have other authority figures in their life that can provide structure, support, and healthy discipline. But seldom can they provide the loving, nurturing, and empathy of a parent. You, as a parent, are the first place your child looks to for that kind of comfort.

Empathy

Once ADHD parents adjust their attitude to view the child from empathy, understanding, and love, they realize the behaviors they find so irritating are frequently their child's way of asking for help. The parent stops taking their child's behavior as something personal and no longer loses their temper.

Your child will benefit from you becoming knowledgeable about ADHD as it is a crucial method of showing your child love and empathy. By making sure they fully comprehend instructions, you will avoid potential conflicts or difficulties in completing tasks.

If your child tells lies often, you can show love and empathy for your child by helping them stop. Perhaps your child is in too many situations that are frustrating and they cannot succeed. You can help the child change the behavior by changing the situation, giving them more opportunities to succeed. When a child begins telling the truth, reward it with praise, affection, or in other ways.

If your ADHD child is forgetful, you can show love and empathy by posting reminders, writing notes, or placing images strategically around the home where your child will notice them. For example, you might stick a reminder on the refrigerator door or the child's backpack. You could write a reminder on a kitchen chalkboard. Perhaps your child is more likely to notice an email or a text message on their phone. All these things will be effective in your child's life.

There are three fundamental types of strategies needed to raise a child with ADHD. Each of them incorporates empathy, love, and compassion. Your capacity to understand and share feelings with your child is empathy. Love is the feeling of deep affection for your child, and compassion is both giving kindness and acceptance to your child. The three types are as follows.

- **Learning:** The Most Helpful Strategy in Parenting Your Child
- **Understand:** Positive Parenting Strategies
- **Read:** A Radically Positive Parenting — A Nurtured Heart Approach

When you show excitement, interest, and empathy for your child, you validate their thoughts and feelings. This is the single most helpful strategy in parenting your ADHD child. Everyone seeks validation when they express their ideas. Parents can sometimes react to their child by being dismissive or by minimizing. Comments like, "You are overreacting," "You act like a baby," or "You are exaggerating" can fuel your child's emotional intensity because they invalidate feelings and thoughts.

They may experience sudden mood swings that make it difficult for you to manage them. The form your child uses to deliver their message to you may not be the least bit pleasant to experience. But even with the rawest emotional outbursts, the child is engaged in an appraisal of their situation, simple assessments of what is happening in the moment. They either express likes or dislikes, wants or don't want. Listening for appraisals and validating them can go a long way toward de-escalating any potential conflict between you and your child.

Positive appraisals (likes, wants) are generally associated with positive emotions (happiness, love, serenity). Negative appraisals (dislikes, rejections) are associated with negative emotions (fear, hate, anger). The appraisal may not always be expressed in words, especially with a young child.

Holding a broken toy, your child may come to you in tears, hoping you will fix it. You can validate his feelings by validating the appraisal, "It is sad that your boat is broken. I have felt like you feel now. When my things break, I am sad too."

That was a simple example. But suppose you are dealing with your ADHD teen. You know the gang engages in some risky behaviors. Your son speaks to you in an anxious tone. He talks fast. He tells you the boys expect him to join. They have said that he will be viewed as a chicken if he refuses.

You are pleased that your son trusts you enough to discuss it with you before deciding, but you also detect some ambiguity in his emotions. A good response should begin with praising your son for trusting you enough to discuss it with you. You remember how important it was to fit in with other guys and to prove yourself.

Then, you might say, "When I was a teen, there were times when I was rebellious and did risky things. Even though I was afraid, I did them anyway. My fear told me I should avoid these things, but I thought they mattered to my friends. But after doing them, I found out they only mattered to me."

If you think your child might join a gang involved in criminal activity, you need to make certain they understand that they will not be permitted. Outline the consequences if your child disobeys. They may not be obvious to your child, who is prone to taking risks. But there is every reason for you to continue discussing the situation as you have your son's attention. Every parent and child will present a diverse set of experiences.

The point is that you, as a parent want to use your experience as much as possible to instruct your child on good behavior. The best possible way to do this is by validating their emotions. Your child will be more receptive to learning from your experience and you will learn more from your child's experience. When you validate your child's thoughts and feelings, you make it possible for dialogue and negotiations in which you can express your own emotions and your concerns for your child.

Positive parenting is a principle of child-rearing based on the premise that every child is born with good intentions and the aspiration to do what is right.

Positive parenting strategies do not entail giving in to a child's unruly behavior or demands. They are not methods for spoiling a child. Following instructions and doing what is expected is something most children can do. But a child with ADHD will have a tough time consistently maintaining attention to tasks when there is no immediate feedback or reward. They need positive reinforcement to feel motivated when tasks are not intrinsically stimulating.

If you desire good behavior, reward that behavior every time you notice it. If you miss a few rewards, it is okay as research shows that intermittent rewards are more effective than continuous ones in reinforcing the good behavior you desire. You reward the behavior with praise each time you observe it. Your ADHD child will learn the behavior through repetition. Positive reinforcement (rewards) will also perpetuate the motivation to continue the behavior in the future. You can gradually phase out your reward system once the desired behavior has become well established.

Positive parenting with an ADHD child is a tough challenge. Most parents of an ADHD child want to do and say things that will improve their child's self-esteem. Is it possible to work on weak points in the child's behavior without lowering the child's self-esteem? Some practical steps are provided in what follows, which can make this go more smoothly.

However, parents need to clearly understand what does not work. Your ADHD child will not respond positively to shouting, spanking, or nagging. These and other negative reinforcing approaches to discipline will tear an ADHD child down, and any sense of self-esteem they have will be lost.

Communication with ADHD Child

As your child matures, they develop their own identity. With individual interests and routines, you are going to be amazed that your little one is now growing and becoming more independent than ever. Although you might feel like you are struggling to keep up, you can even it out if you learn how to communicate effectively. When you speak to your child with ADHD, remember that listening is also an active role. Both of you must feel like you are being understood and respected during each interaction. Being an active listener and clear communicator will enhance your relationship with your child while also helping to overcome their ADHD symptoms that desire to push you away.

Do not take it personally if you notice your child starts pushing you away. Even without ADHD in the picture, this is a natural part of growing up. They are seeking more independence, which is a positive trait because this is how they will learn to fend for themselves in the real world.

As a parent, you must walk a narrow line between allowing your children to grow and fully stepping away from your responsibilities as a parent. This will simply push them away and make them wary of engaging in conversation.

ADHD can cause your child to be talkative at times and introspective at others. Do not take this to heart because they do not mean to only do this to you. This is the way their brain processes life, and you already know what you can do to help to make this easier for them. All you can do is being there when they want your help, love, guidance, and advice. If you need to step in to teach them a lesson or to discipline them, you will also be there to do so. Otherwise, you need to let your child live and learn a bit. This is how you raise a healthy child who is ready to grow up and take care of themselves.

No matter how old they are now, this time will feel like it is passing quickly. You need to hold on to all the precious moments that you have before they slip through your fingers. Pretty soon, your child will be the one cooking for you and teach you knew things that they learned in school. They will be the ones asking if they can drive around and do things independently. While they are still reliant on you, this is the prime opportunity for you to make sure that you are there for them. Use your excellent communication skills to make them feel comfortable enough to approach you for any reason.

The Keys to Communication

When you think about the term "communication," you probably think about speaking. This is one part of communicating, but it is not the only part. Great communication skills include active listening and speaking. Your child will need to be heard sometimes, and they will not always need you to respond with tips or advice. A reaction is likely all that they need because it shows them that you care about what is happening to them. By following these tips, you are going to become a much better communicator and have a better relationship with your child with ADHD.

Make Sure They Feel Loved and Accepted

When your child chooses to communicate with you, appreciate the time and courage that it took them to make this decision. It is not always easy to talk to your parents, especially if you are young and intimidated. There is a lot changing for a child as they grow up, and they likely have many questions that you have the answers to as their guardian. Make sure that you let them know how much you love and accept them, even when they mess up. And they will make mistakes, but it should not change the way that you treat them.

If you always surround your child with reminders of love and acceptance, you will find that they will be more likely to come to you for the important matters, good or bad. They will be excited to tell you when great things happen to them and when they learn something new. On the other hand, they will feel comfortable talking to you about what is wrong and what is bothering them.

As they grow older, they are probably going to feel self-conscious about their condition and wish that they could just be "normal." When you remind them how special they are and all the skills they have, you reinforce the point that they are still smart and worthy. Intelligence is not only measured by test scores and grades. You need to validate your child to let them know that they are good enough.

Treating ADHD as a part of life and not acting like it is a flaw is the best approach you can take. Your child will relax and accept themselves just as much as you and your partner accept them. There might be bullies along the way who try to tell them otherwise, but you can rid them of these negative thinking patterns by reinforcing the point that they are amazing and have so much to offer the world. As their parent, you get to build them up and make sure that their self-esteem continues to grow.

Pick Discussion Times Wisely

There is not always going to be the perfect time and place to have a serious discussion, especially when your child is actively misbehaving. You might be in public or around other people who you would rather not hear the conversation. You can let them know that you need to have a talk later, but do not fully engage until you are able to be in an environment that is private and stable.

Your child is going to react defiantly because of their ADHD if you try to reason with them in public or in front of others. Some might act out even more to show off to those in the area. ADHD can turn your child into quite the entertainer, and that is only going to frustrate and discourage you. You must exercise your patience before you engage in a serious conversation like this.

By telling your child you need to talk when you get home, they are still going to realize the seriousness of the situation. This will not ruin their current experience, but you are planting the seed in their mind that a talk is coming, so they need to prepare to communicate with you. Teach them that this does not have to be a scary thing because this does not always result in punishment.

One of the worst things for your child's ADHD is interruptions because this will break their concentration. If a distraction enters the room or space that you are in while you are communicating, they could lose interest entirely. This is not what you want, and then you will need to have the conversation all over again.

Let Your Child Know They Are Not Alone

There are many who have ADHD, and it will help your child to know they aren't alone, as they may not have considered that. Talk about the fact that having ADHD is not weird or bad. They don't have anything wrong with them; rather, they have some unique challenges to face as they grow up. You can also mention that adults have ADHD. If you have it as well, this is a great conversation starter because you use that as an example to relate to your child in a way that no one else can. If you know the symptoms just as well, you should be able to offer your insight and some great advice—this will make for some great communication.

Having any kind of disorder makes you feel different, and this can be frustrating and lonely. Remind your child that not everybody is educated on the topic, but that does not mean it cannot change. Help them to figure out ways to explain to others what ADHD feels like because hearing it from the source is important. It is the most eye-opening way to receive this information.

Do Not Expect Instant Interest

When you have more frequent conversations with your child, do not feel offended if they do not show immediate interest in what you have to say. Also, do not feel bad if they refuse to open to you. The process of communication can take time, with and without ADHD. Children usually go through phases where they want to talk all the time, and others where they don't.

Chapter 9:
How ADHD Impacts on Family Members

A DHD may change routines and relationships that affect the entire family, not just the person with the illness. Being a caregiver for someone with ADHD may be demanding and frustrating.

The disease impacts not just children with ADHD. Households with an ADHD child frequently experience greater stress and annoyance than families without a child with ADHD. Everything from relationships to family finances might suffer because of this. Even the parents' decision to have more children may be impacted.

More effort and direction are needed while providing daily care for a child with ADHD. One parent might need to give up their job and take care of the child full-time at home, a decision that impacts the family's income. Parents with children with ADHD may be unable to participate in activities outside the house due to the increased demands on their time and resources.

The problems that might result from having a child with ADHD can also strain the marriage or relationship between the parents. Conversely the struggle may deepen family ties as parents work together.

According to studies, having an ADHD patient in the family might impact how happy parents, siblings, and other family members are with their daily lives. For instance, children with ADHD place significantly more demands on the time and attention of parents. That may cause issues in relationships, less family time spent together, and an increase in conflict. According to research, parents of children with ADHD experience divorce and depression at greater rates than parents without a child with ADHD.

However, you may take action to ensure that everything continues to flow as smoothly as possible for everyone. Although it takes some getting used to, some resources are always available.

In Terms of Parental Skills

Another way ADHD can hit grown-ups is by decreasing their parental abilities. Surveys indicate that the ADHD manifestations in children made guardians feel helpless, and they were more careless in their nurturing and prone to overreacting. Researchers likewise observed that these guardians did not feel the pressure to keep up with discipline practices and showed less successful critical thinking practices in raising a child with ADHD.

The connection between parental practices and ADHD is worth considering for controlling guardians' mental stress. Researchers have determined that poor nurturing by guardians with ADHD children may be a reason for the parental strain connected with raising youngsters with difficulties such as ADHD. However, when one parent has ADHD, especially the mother, there are more difficulties.

The manifestations of ADHD in guardians frequently lead to reduced self-confidence in nurturing skills and a feeling that they do not have control over the situation. In women with ADHD who are pregnant for the first time, there are often negative emotions concerning their ability to parent effectively.

Paternal ADHD, then again, may cause lower academic performance, even in children who do not have ADHD. This information demonstrates that the limited confidence and instructive capacities of guardians with ADHD are not simply a response to the expanding requests brought up by their child with ADHD.

In many cases, guardians with ADHD know that their nurturing abilities are insufficient. They may even express their sentiments and feelings regarding this inadequacy to their spouse or trusted friend.

This admission may create an additional decrease in their parental abilities.

In Terms of Inheritability

When it comes to inheritability, adults with ADHD are at greater risk of having a child with ADHD than adults who do not have ADHD. The circumstance is the other way around, which implies that ADHD youngsters put their parents in danger of fostering a comparative condition. According to research, around one-fourth of children with ADHD have one parent with ADHD.

While ADHD in guardians is related to ADHD in children, there are no contrasts between children with diligent versus dispatched ADHD guardians. Essentially, parental ADHD doesn't mean that a child will have advanced ADHD. In fact, research seems to indicate that nature and nurture both impact these children.

In Terms of Psychiatric Disorders

Children and teens who have ADHD can influence the psychological well-being of their parents and guardians, who are more likely to struggle with mental issues. This pattern indicates that raising a child with ADHD may cause depression in parents.

In Terms of Parental Resources

Research has uncovered that raising a child with ADHD challenges the parents' emotional and physical resources. Additionally, parents of a child with ADHD will fight more often.

Parents of children with ADHD often act out because of the pressure they feel. They may experience chronic anxiety and mental strain because of stress of managing their child's disease. Some are easily dissatisfied, engage in risky behavior, alcohol abuse, are quick to anger, distracted, and easily frustrated.

Ultimately, the troublesome conduct combined with the side effects of ADHD weakens of the family's ability to function well. Parents with ADHD have a more difficult time raising their child with ADHD. All parents are at a greater risk of stress, anxiety, and depression because of the challenges in raising a child with ADHD.

In Terms of Siblings

ADHD appears to significantly affect the other children in the household. One of the most well-known issues called attention to siblings of children with ADHD is the disruption cause by the one with ADHD. Some examples described include:

- Verbal aggression
- Emotional immaturity
- Physical aggression
- Poor academic performance
- Social immaturity
- Family conflicts
- Poor peer relationships.

Siblings of ADHD patients portray their day-to-day life as tumultuous. Some have said that every part of their lives revolves around their sibling with ADHD, and many are never certain what's in store, and don't see ADHD not affecting their lives in some way.

There are three ways that siblings of children with ADHD see the impact of that child's behavior, including caretaking, exploitation, or the sensation of misfortune or distress. They typically feel misled because of verbal hostility, physical fights, and controlling behavior from that sibling. Many believe that their parents do not protect them from their sibling with ADHD, and the parents concede that they don't have the energy to intervene.

Additional distress emerges when parents ask an older sibling to watch their sibling with ADHD. They may be asked to babysit, dispense medication, help with homework, and intervene with teachers and other children. While some siblings will feel pride at being allowed to help, others feel put upon. They help their parents, but the help isn't reciprocated. Siblings of children with ADHD feel unlucky and long for a quiet, more normal life. They wish for more attention from their parents.

Some are disappointed in how much their sibling with ADHD impacts their everyday life. They accept that their family can't have the same adventures as other "normal" families, from vacations to trips to the grocery store. They may also think that because of how they feel, they don't deserve their parents' time and attention.

To summarize, the impacts of ADHD are not restricted to a solitary individual. It spreads throughout the family and impacts all in it.

Chapter 10:
ADHD at School

When your child reaches the age of six and starts school, his symptoms become more apparent, and can also negatively affect his life. Insisting on structure in your child's day and establishing a routine is particularly helpful in school. Although it has nothing to do with his level of intelligence and ADHD is not technically a learning disability, your child with ADHD will likely struggle at school.

He will have to wake up early and learn a new morning routine when he probably only just began to master the old one. He will have to worry about sitting still, paying attention in a classroom, and remembering and following complex instructions. He will also have to interact with other children in social situations, which is sometimes the most difficult challenge they face.

For your child to flourish at school, there must be a collaboration between the teachers, school administrators, and you as parents. Work with your child's teachers and counselors to help him learn to control the disorder and enable him to glean as much from the school experience as possible. Teachers should be well-informed about the child's condition so everyone can be on the same page regarding his needs. Initially, your child may need help coping with school life because sitting still will be difficult. He may walk around at inappropriate times and say inappropriate things.

He will also forget to record homework assignments and test dates. Because he won't always pay attention, he may not know about upcoming activities unless the teacher writes them down in his notebook. He will be distracted by what other students in the class are doing or by something happening outside.

Ensure that everyone is working with the same educational goals for your child. Call a meeting with all parties to address the situation if they are not. You can also ask for the child's therapist to be present so that to advise the teachers on best practices that will benefit your child.

Be prepared to spend many evenings doing homework with your child, who will most likely take a lot longer to complete than his siblings and other children in his class. He will need you to help him stay focused and minimize distractions.

There are laws in place that state your child cannot be discriminated against in education because he has a disorder and that provisions must be made to help him succeed. These provisions may include (but are not limited to) the delivery method, preferred seating, and extra time to complete work. Your child will qualify for these special considerations once it is proved that his disorder limits his ability to function at school. In short, do as much as possible to ensure that your child receives the best education possible to enable him to reach his full potential.

Ask the teacher to keep you informed about what occurs in the classroom, whether your child is disruptive or not. Regular updates keep you informed and enable you to decide whether he needs additional therapy or exercise.

If he isn't already sitting up front, ask the teacher to move him where she can tell if he is paying attention and pull him back when he starts daydreaming or is distracted by other stimuli.

It is also important to let the teachers and school officials know that you have educational expectations for your child. Ask teachers for input regarding how reasonable those expectations are and welcome their advice and recommendations. At the same time, be alert for signs that the school has given up on your child and speak to the teachers about it immediately. If both teams are not working in tandem, the child will not flourish in that atmosphere.

As stated previously, establish a special place at home for homework. It should be quiet with no distractions. The television should be off or out of hearing; siblings should be in another room if possible. If small children are in the home require supervision, have the other parent or other family members watch them until homework time is over. Make it clear to the child that he must record his homework assignments, as they will likely forget.

While you will need to help with homework, resist the urge to do it for him, although you might assist by making the instructions simpler so that he can follow them. It might help to divide the assignments into more manageable portions, so your child does not feel overwhelmed. Take breaks as needed so that he has an opportunity to refocus.

As a parent of a child with ADHD you would probably have to buy extra school supplies such as pens pencils and erasers, because children with ADHD tend to forget things and are usually unorganized.

Helping your child perform well at school is a significant part of coping with ADHD.

Bullying

While many children with ADHD are teased about their condition at school, some believe that children with ADHD are likely to become bullies for various reasons. Children with ADHD struggle academically and combined with common frustrations; they may show it by bullying other children. Because they are not empathetic, they do not feel guilty taking advantage of another child to stop feeling bad about themselves and their inability to fit in. Medication would not make a difference in this scenario, as the stimulants usually given to children with ADHD do not weaken the aggression they feel.

You can help to decrease or stop the bullying habits of your child by letting him know in a calm, unemotional tone that you have been informed about their behavior. You must impress upon him that while you love him unconditionally, his behavior is unacceptable. Tell him that if the behavior continues, there will be consequences just as there have always been for poor behavior. The parent should also work with the child's teacher to find something for the child to do at school to occupy his time and give him a sense of responsibility and purpose. Perhaps he can do simple clerical tasks for another teacher. He will feel less need to work off aggression if he is busy completing a job he has been entrusted to carry out.

Another proactive action would be to take him out of situations where he is likely to bully other children, such as during lunch or after school. Teachers can ensure that the child spends this time in a supervised location.

Outside of school, you can engage him in role-play sessions where you teach him to respond to situations without resorting to bullying. For a severe case, you might ask his counselor to help him with anger management strategies to teach him to control his emotions before they get to the point of violence.

When you find out your child may be bullying, don't lose your temper and scream and shout at your child. Never resort to a violent punishment such as spanking because that would confuse the child; how can you teach that violence is unacceptable by being violent yourself? Your child is not bullying other children because you failed as a parent, so don't react by making excuses for his behavior and finding fault with your own. That would be counterproductive and will not do anything to alleviate the behavior.

It is interesting to note that although children with ADHD tend to become bullies more frequently than other children, they are also most likely to have been bullied at some point. When this happens, it usually increases their symptoms, so talk to your child if you hear or believe he is being bullied before he gets to the point of frustration that causes him to be bullied himself. Talk to the teachers at his school about what is happening so they can act. If needed, remove him from the situation. Be there for him so his self-esteem does not suffer.

Self-Esteem

Children with ADHD are often kept apart from others because they are considered disruptive. They might fight, bully other children, or resort to disruptive behavior. As a result, they spend a lot of time alone. Even for events such as birthday parties and other gatherings, children with ADHD might be left out because they are indifferent at a time in their lives when children want to fit in. These forms of rejection can lower a child's self-esteem. As a parent, it is up to you to balance these negative occurrences by praising your child and rewarding them whenever they do well in school or social situations. It could be for doing something as simple as hanging up his clothes or something more significant such as doing well on a test at school.

Apart from praising them for good behavior, let your child know that you love him unconditionally and remind him about everything about him that is good and valuable. Ensure any criticism is constructive and enhances rather than detracts from his self-esteem. Criticize the behavior, not your child. Stay calm. If, after repeated attempts, you believe that you cannot raise your child's self-esteem on your own, seek professional help. If you think training might help, there are organizations, such as Children and Adults with Attention Deficit/Hyperactivity Disorder (CHADD), which offer programs for parents.

Chapter 11:
Managing ADHD Behavior Away from Home

You can't stay home indefinitely, so handling ADHD behavior in the outside world is crucial. It can be dangerous to travel. If you do not carefully manage your child's actions, you may not accomplish all you had hoped. Worse, your child might have a melt-down and cause damage or hurt someone, and it can be costly. When she handles herself, it's perfect. How do you help her behave when you're away from home?

Problems in the Car

The relationship you build with your child will help wherever you go, especially when issues arise in the car. It is both aggravating and risky to drive if your child is misbehaving. You may be in a rush sometimes, and if your child isn't in the mood, she will slow you down.

Solutions

You want your daughter to put on her seat belt without being told to do so, but if she's upset with something else, she may refuse to cooperate. Rather than focus on her noncompliance, root out the source of her annoyance.

Because the backseat can be lonely, talk with her and include her in conversations. Pack items of interest to her or play a game to make the trip less lonely and boring.

When driving, if your child acts out, you may be worried she will hurt herself or someone else in the car. The best option may be to pull over. Yes, perhaps you're late, but it's the best option. Once safely stopped, say, "You have to be calm so that it is safe for me to drive the car." When you resume your trip, ensure the children do something quietly, even if it's looking out the window. The fighting can resume quickly if they are not distracted from the conflict.

Who Sits Where?

When there is constant disagreement over the seating arrangement in the car, apply the same techniques that you would use to minimize conflict within the household; help the children figure out the sharing system they want to use. Do this before your next trip: ask the children if they have any suggestions to fix the problem at a time when everyone is calm. Every child may have a special seating choice, but everything will be fine if they find out what works for them.

Using the Bathroom

Accessing clean rest areas and public toilets on a long trip can be challenging. Your daughter may insist that she doesn't have to go to the bathroom before you leave, but she may complain that she needs the toilet shortly after you leave the house. You will have to stop but try to find a solution that reduces the discomfort if the situation is routine. Let her know: "It's a long trip and finding a bathroom will be hard. Want to use the bathroom now to make you more relaxed while we're driving?" If she says no, you might add, "We'd be happy to wait for you," to make her rethink.

Help your child get into the bathroom routine before leaving—model what you'd like her to do and ask if she'd like to take a turn. There may be a considerable difficulty if events play poorly but try to stay relaxed as she pays attention to her discomfort. She will eventually learn that she's better off following your suggestion, and you don't have to say any more about it.

Problems in the Store

If you're looking for something she likes, your daughter may be cooperative. But when she feels compelled to buy for others, her behavior may be different. As is often the case, once she lacks the authority to determine what happens, her ADHD behaviors may spark and intensify.

Solutions

If you're in a good mood, your child will be as well, so you have significant influence. Talking about her favorite topics can also help make unnecessary shopping less annoying. An even better solution would be to involve her in the process. Whether you are shopping for groceries or a gift for a friend she knows and likes, ask for her input. Older children might be happy to help you find bargains. Others may want to read the list of groceries or push the cart.

The bottom line is that when you and your child interact positively and share authority, ADHD behaviors will be less frequent. Look for the "sweet spot" where you have the time to do what you need. Although hard, it is possible, and during shopping excursions, this has the biggest long-term effect on the rate of ADHD behavior.

Resolving Public Misbehavior

When you're out and about, things may not always go smoothly. So, what's the plan when your child misbehaves? If necessary, you should disregard or avoid the actions, but encouraging it is not acceptable. There may also be dangers when she's exuberant in public places that you don't want to play out.

Sadly, once her conduct is disrespectful or dangerous, you may have to physically stop her or leave the store. In some situations, after a short time, it may be possible to re-enter the shop if your child settles down and you feel confident that you have resolved the situation.

However, there are times when you will have to return later. In these cases, your child must understand that her behaviors have a ripple effect in these circumstances. Highlight the negative side effects. You might say, "Because we haven't done our shopping, we're going to have to go back later, and I'm not going to be able to make the dessert

I was preparing for tonight." If the problem continues, you might take it further by suggesting that your daughter spend some of her own money to pay for the return trip. Point out that she is offering compensation for interrupting the day with her behavior.

Like when dealing with hygiene issues, you might ask your child if she'd like to stay home next time and use some of her money to pay someone to keep her company. This way, she understands the responsibility of refusing to satisfy the family's agenda. Offer her choices, but also let her know it may cost her.

Peer Relationships

Is your child trying to "buy" friends by giving away personal items? Is she displaying low self-esteem? Does she want you to run interference when friends aren't treating her the way she wants? Will she always sit on the playground by herself or just play with children out of the common circle?

You want a fun social life for your child and feel comfortable interacting with a variety of people.

Misbehaving with Peers

Quite often, when a child with ADHD meets another rambunctious child, her behavior digresses. She believes that she will stop feeling inferior if she acts in ways she knows aren't acceptable, especially if the others are behaving in the same way. There is power in numbers, and when she teams up with a "bad friend," your daughter gathers influence and leverage.

Solutions

You can try to keep your child away from others who act out. This can, however, give her the impression that she is weak and easily manipulated.

Another alternate approach is to explain the flaws in her thought process and help her handle what happens when she faces negative influences successfully. This approach offers her the opportunity to be a leader and influencer. You might say, "Your friend might be clever enough to imitate you when you're playing together."

You might also ask your daughter how she feels about getting in trouble and ask, "How do you want others to see you?" You can help her work out what to do when others push the envelope. She may be fearful that others will make fun of her if she doesn't join. They may be pushing the limits to gain attention or weaken the adults' authority.

Doubting Acceptability

If your daughter doubts others accept her, she will find it harder to act correctly. Perhaps when she clowns around, she makes others laugh, but an unfortunate side effect is that she receives attention for immature behavior. She takes advantage of habits that will not serve her well.

If that's the case, you might say, "Do you believe you're going to have to show off or do something silly for people to like you?" Then ask, "How is this going to work for you?" When she thinks it goes poorly, ask her, "I wonder if there are other ways to attract them?"

You want to maintain your child's great sense of humor, but you don't want her to be crazy or dumb. She has many qualities others will admire, and you want her to bring them out. Her actions with ADHD diminish significantly when she is socially comfortable and confident that she is accepted as she is. Additionally, her choice of friends will likely change if she feels good about herself.

Supporting Social Development

If your child is younger, she'll repeat the same behaviors with other family members that she uses with you. If she is demanding and possessive with you, so will also be that way with her playmates. When family members manipulate her or are disrespectful, or others give her a hard time, she may overreact or be afraid. It is important to nurture habits that fit well with non-family members for these reasons. If you want her to communicate, accept social boundaries, and conduct with her peers assertively, improve her ability to connect within the group.

It is also helpful to allow your child to interact with other children while encouraging their social development. So, she's going to increase her social skills. Encourage her efforts and say, "Let me know when you want to bring someone over so we can make arrangements for a play date."

You might discover that your daughter wants to interact with younger children as she enjoys social power or the ability to regress and behave more childishly. You may also note that she is searching for older children who introduce her to new things and care for her. Yet make sure that she also interacts with children her age, as this provides more ways to solve issues relating to sharing and rivalry. And in her classroom, she will have to work with this age group.

Equally important, before you speak to her about her social interactions, give your child plenty of opportunity to decide what is fair and reasonable. This time allows her to determine what she will and won't accept in social settings. Help her find a good way to solve her social dilemmas. You may ask, for example, "Is your friend shouting to get you to do what she wants?" As with manners, she becomes more socially adept each time she seeks a workable solution.

Problems When You Visit with Others

It is both fun and challenging to raise a child. Being a parent can feel overwhelming when the child misbehaves because of ADHD. If you feel helpless and isolated, your situation will deteriorate significantly. You may want to socialize with adult friends, but your child's actions can make social visits almost impossible.

If your child is used to being the focus of your life, it is possible she uses behaviors common to children with ADHD to keep your focus on her. She always does something to bring you back when you're distracted by something else. If you take her on a casual outing, plan to relax and enjoy your friend's company for a few minutes, she'll make sure you don't forget her. She might cause a scene: tug on your arm and interrupt your conversation. She climbs on you or makes a mess to pull you away from your friend. You are constantly distracted by the fact that you must listen to her. You feel embarrassed, and conversation is impossible.

The situation worsens when she overhears you mention her poor behavior. Now the conversation is about her and what she needs, not about what you, as a parent and adult, need. And if you cut your stay short, you reinforce her behavior, and she will continue to misbehave to bring the attention back to her.

Solutions

It's not only good for you to get your daughter to comply during social interactions, but it's also good for her. If she's going to be successful with teachers and others, she's going to have to learn not to be the center of attention. She must adapt and share the spotlight. A social trip to another person's home requires all these things, so practicing those positive habits is a great opportunity for your child.

Wanting to Quit Group Activities

You will want to include your child in organized groups and extracurricular activities, as it supports children's physical and social growth and encourages discipline. It often takes money and effort on your part. Despite the drain on you financially and emotionally, you may find that leaving is not an option: you want her to recognize the importance of meeting commitments, building inner strength, and learning to solve head-on issues.

To do that, you may push her with consequences if she doesn't fulfill her obligations for a scheduled event. Her teammates are counting on her, she agreed, and it's good for her. Your child may sometimes give in to your demands and continue to attend.

But the way things are handled may not always work well. She may go through the motions and hardly try, and she may be humiliated by her actions. The circumstances may feel like a tragedy because you want a good experience for her, but all you get are complaints.

Solutions

You can talk to your child about the impact of her actions on the other team members who rely on her continued involvement. You can also ask, "If you really want to quit, will you call (coach, instructor, or planner) to say you're quitting?" This tactic may inspire her to keep up with the activity.

But a reluctance to leave may mean that the event disappoints your child. It can mean that she overreacts to a lack of success, receives negative comments from the sidelines, or is scared. It may also mean she will threaten you or feel compelled to participate. She will be hesitant to continue to participate unless these issues are resolved.

Find a Comfortable Resolution

Your goal is to help your child feel confident enough to tell you what's troubling her. You may ask, "What makes it hard for you to be there?" She may need to work her way up to it, so don't ask her to get straight to the point.

The solution is easy at times. You may ask another child, for instance, to tutor your child so that she can become more proficient at a sport or craft without an audience. You could encourage her to watch other children and see how it is done. Or you might ask her to mentor a less-talented girl, which would improve her sense of ability.

Nevertheless, your child may continue to resist. You should split the task into less daunting phases when that happens to keep training environments as non-threatening as possible to help acclimatize her. But let her know that depression won't help her if she wants to feel better.

Teach about Making Commitments

Your child may have signed on for a sports league without paying enough attention to what she agreed. Maybe she quits when she finds a problem, a waste of money.

If this happens often, you may need to limit what you're willing to fund. If she signs up for soccer, make her agree that no matter the problem, she must play the entire season. But she doesn't have to play again if she doesn't want to play. If she takes an art class, she must give it a specific period before she can drop out.

Whatever the restrictions, they are necessary because spending money unnecessarily is not okay. So let your child know she will have to pay a percentage of the fee before she signs up again. You can always pay her back at that time if she fulfills the duty. You want her to have something riding on finishing what she starts.

However, be advised: if your child can't get out of something that sincerely doesn't suit her, your discipline may backfire. Trying something new will raise her resistance, and you want her to be excited and daring. You don't want to think that she's stuck and awkward. If she can't get out, she might not get in and learn to avoid enriching and beneficial activities. You don't want to associate commitments with negativity.

Chapter 12:
The Five Reinforcements for ADHD Behavior

Y oung children are self-centered. They are weak, and they rely on others for protection and assistance. They need to be able to command the attention of their caregivers. Many hyperactive or impulsive habits also need reinforcement: these behaviors usually draw people and make things happen fast.

As children grow older, it is expected that they will have more control over themselves and will follow many rules. They continue to chafe their actions at these restrictions, and this is when inattention can be exacerbated as a way for the big kid to avoid accountability.

In other words, actions driven by ADHD (hyperactivity, impulsiveness, and inattentiveness) can lead to outcomes that relieve your child's distress. They can also prompt you and others to pay more attention and support to your child. When you understand what strengthens the behavior of ADHD, you can change the effects of this kind of behavior to reduce its frequency. You will help your child learn different habits with fewer negative side effects, which produce better outcomes.

Attention

Your child may become rambunctious the moment you start talking to a friend. It's possible that this happens because your relationship with someone makes your child nervous. He continues to target things off-limits or make a noise as soon as your attention shifts away from him. Such habits have the important effect of making you know what they're doing. Sometimes a familiar expression or facial movement is all it takes to allow him to attempt to replicate this form of ADHD activity.

Behaviors of ADHD can be effective ways to keep the child centered. When he is busy, hyperactive, insane, annoying, or distracting, it's hard to separate from your child. It can be an effective way to get your mind to move by putting items next to your head or flopping randomly on your lap while you speak to someone.

Off-task activities attract attention at school and at home. If your child is floundering, fiddling, or not following instructions, others may feel compelled to connect with and remain with him until he complies. This reassures the child that other people are concerned about him and care about him. This neglect may lead to support and motivational opportunities, and he may like it when a person repeats his name or pleads for an answer. His actions can even win him a seat next to you or the instructor.

Waiting rooms and other public spaces are fertile ground for an activity that attracts publicity because your child has a captive audience. This ADHD behavior will begin if you read a magazine to pass the time. Your child isn't mean; he just wants your attention. There are many drawbacks to being loud and crazy. The one that is most noticed is often the loudest and most bizarre person in the room. Shouting can be a way to increase the probability of a response; clowning can be amusing, and when others listen, it is generally harder for parents to impose restrictions.

People might say your child can't help himself, but we can't ignore the effects of intense behaviors, which is more apparent when the child is talking and thinking aloud. The constant chatter stops them from feeling lonely, and when you hear a running joke, you wonder what he's doing. His talk and noise stream keeps you both connected. Although he may go off on tangents, there's no room for anyone else to talk about his never-ending story.

Accommodation

ADHD activity also leads to unnecessary social accommodations. For example, if your child creates a scene because he wants you to leave, you will unwittingly strengthen his impatience when you hurry along. If your child forces you to get something special to calm him down, the effect of his poor behavior is that he gets more. Even if you're threatening to punish, until you spend extra time and energy, he's still learning not to comply. ADHD will work well to get you to give more, do more, and work harder.

Another example of this problem occurs when your child is inattentive and then relies on you to tell him what's happening. He's likely to fail if he does this at school, as his teachers will only have time to get him up to speed sometimes.

Your child may relate love to rescue as well. If he moves into difficult or dangerous circumstances, your attempts to keep him from harm will remind him that he is valuable to you. And this involves reminders of his basic needs, which is making allowances for his bad behavior.

The accommodated child often asks questions about things he can easily solve independently. He loves the fact that you abandon everything to answer his questions. Playing dumb will raise assistance because it's hard to enforce conditions, keep him accountable, or encourage him to help if you have concerns about his performance. His ineffectiveness will leave you concerned about him, and overcoming his trials and tribulations is your duty. He also complains, "Why have you not told me?" when you didn't interfere. When you and others "pick up the slack," the side effect is that he's unqualified.

Avoidance

To children and adults alike, avoidance is a common way to cope with adversity. Avoidance benefits can perpetuate distractibility and lack of focus and listening, which are the hallmarks of ADHD. However, we don't achieve control because we ignore it, and the question never goes away. Ultimately, it is not safe for us to hide our heads in the sand.

Once a child is diagnosed with ADHD, most people no longer attempt to understand his actions as an inability to cooperate, attend, or adapt. They conclude that when we talk to him, his ADHD stops him from paying attention. They think he can't learn to stop and listen to what you're doing. If he continues to play and fails to respond to your demands, they presume it is because he is hyper-focused pathologically. People will stop saying he hates you; they will blame his lack of courtesy and sensitivity on ADHD instead.

But all these distracted responses also have benefits. These can often protect your child from danger and encourage him to continue with his mission. He may feel others are not listening, so in return, he stops listening. Instead, he tunes out or yawns when others are critical or demanding. It involves changing the topic when they press him to discuss certain topics. And it involves daydreaming and not acknowledging others.

Instead of having a disability, your child may have discovered that he doesn't have to adhere to the conditions you enforce if he doesn't react. Distractibility gives him more time to do what he wants. It allows him to float away in imagination.

Distractibility prevents a child from pain of all sorts. It takes him away from assessment, punishment, and restriction-related conditions. His absorption in his thinking and actions saves him from unpleasant things, like too simple or repetitive activities.

As soon as he feels you're nagging or lecturing, your child may become lethargic and adopt a weary expression. Many people know how difficult it is to listen to extended speech without getting a chance to get feedback. If the lesson goes on long enough, many with ADHD will tune out. Such sorts of responses are shown often and rapidly in children with ADHD.

Acquisition

Many ADHD-based actions allow a child to get things faster. The sayings "Strike while the iron is hot" and "Take it while you can" demonstrate the advantages of urgent action. Often the child who behaves quickly won't miss out because it's hard for others to block swift and aggressive goal-oriented actions, such as moving forward to get the biggest piece of cake. Some ADHD behaviors will discourage others from refusing your child what they want to deny him. If he acts quickly, your child will easily get what he wants.

If children pick, harass inappropriately, behave rudely, act recklessly, or inflict discomfort on others, we don't like it. But when they work so well, it's hard to get these habits to end. Your child will ping-pong around the house in search of excitement, just as you do while channeling surfing. Generally, ADHD actions will speed things up and break side barriers to help your child find pleasure quicker. Impulsive behavior makes it hard for others to predict their decisions and prevent them from getting what they want.

Your child may also gain a sense of prestige by blurring out what others are afraid to say. It's not that he lacks a filter; his actions enhance his life. Although you encourage respectful behavior, sometimes, when your child's impolite, he loses out less often, and sometimes it's better to apologize than to ask for permission. Adults may think the child cannot the ability to delay gratification or worry about it before he behaves, but it's just his ADHD behavior that works too well.

Your child should enjoy the fun of getting what he wants, even if negative consequences come down the line. The actions become even more valuable when others save them or smooth things over when there are future problems. It is, therefore, important to determine how often people save him before concluding that his rashness is a symptom of illness.

Antagonism

Your child might want to strike back when he is angry or upset. While some children fight for themselves assertively or actively in reaction to confrontation, children living with ADHD are usually more subtle. They could, for example, flip small objects in your face or play with a household item recklessly. We call them impulsive actions, but they serve a purpose. They leave you annoyed, and that's good for the children.

In this situation, the bigger the response to his actions—the more exasperated and frustrated you are—the more likely he will replicate the behavior. Your child will learn precisely how to "push your buttons." For instance, once your child becomes upset that he is expected to wait for an appointment, he will threaten your peace of mind with his humiliating actions. While you may think he's "spacing out" out because he can't control his impulses, it may be that his actions depress you and make you unhappy.

It's not that he's incapable of behaving; by making a scene, he keeps you off balance and disrupts you. He will flail around and repeatedly touch what you forbid him to touch. All these acts can be irritating, and they can serve as revenge. He knows you're disturbed by his unruly public behavior, so he deliberately misbehaves to goad you to act.

Chapter 13:
Improving Social Skills of Children with ADHD

C hildren with ADHD find it difficult to make friends and establish relationships. Some parents wonder how their child's social skills can be developed but often don't know where to start.

All children need positive peer relationships and friendships. However, most children with ADHD have a hard time making friends and being included in the wider peer group. Often, hyperactivity, inattention, and impulsiveness can disrupt a child's attempt at connecting with the people around them in a positive way.

Too often, they do not feel as though they do not belong and are not accepted. Additionally, ADHD can leave a child feeling different and isolated, and these feelings may carry through to adulthood, often with disastrous effects on their future attempts at making friends and forming connections. Children with ADHD are no different than children without; all of them want to be liked, want to be part of a group, and want to make friends. They just do not know how.

Increasing a Child's Social Awareness

According to various research on ADHD, children with this disorder can be poor monitors of their social behavior. They may think a peer interaction went well, but the other person did not think that was the case. This example highlights the fact that the child with ADHD may be unable to accurately read social situations, self-monitor, or adjust their actions and behaviors according to the social setting. These skills must be taught directly.

Often, they react without thinking, but one of the ways to remedy this is to continually provide feedback immediately whenever a child's behavior is inappropriate or he misreads a social cue. Role-play is an extremely effective and helpful way of shaping, teaching, and practicing positive social skills and providing the child with ways to deal with difficult situations, such as bullying and teasing.

As a parent, you can start by focusing on one or two main areas that your child struggles with most regarding social interactions. Starting small creates a learning process that is not too overwhelming for the child or parent.

Often, children with ADHD have problems with the fundamentals of social exchanges, such as:

- Starting and maintaining a conversation
- Interacting with people in a proper way
- Personal distance when talking
- Giving and receiving input
- Listening and asking for ideas
- Taking turns talking in a conversation
- Showing interest
- Negotiating and resolving a conflict
- Speaking using a normal tone.

Identify your child's social rules and behaviors clearly and give them information. Practice these prosocial abilities repeatedly. With immediate rewards, this will form positive behaviors.

Building Friendship Growth Opportunities

For elementary and preschool children, playdates offer a great opportunity for parents to model and coach positive peer interactions for them. The child would be able to practice these new skills. You can set up these playtimes with one or two friends at a time. Keep it minimal rather than having a large group of friends, as this may be overwhelming for the child and you. Plan playtime to be the most effective for your child.

Consider yourself as your child's "friendship mentor" and how long a playdate takes. Select activities that are most interesting for your child.

The older the child gets, friendships and peer relationships become complicated but continue to remain involved in your child's life and help them facilitate interactions that are positive for themselves. The middle and high school years can be harsh for a child who struggles socially. It would be good if your child has at least one or two good friends throughout the years of school that can often be the child's support system rather than having a large group of friends.

Socially alienated secondary school students who face constant rejection may feel desperate to become members of any peer group, including those with adverse impacts.

Another way to foster positive peer relationships outside of school is to get involved in groups within the community, such as Indian Guides, Boy Scouts, Girl Scouts, Girls Who Code, Rotary Club for children, sports teams, and art groups. When getting your children to join these clubs and teams, ensure that group leaders or mentors know about ADHD and create an environment that is both encouraging and constructive for your child.

Don't be worried or afraid to share information about your child's condition with teachers, coaches, and parents in the community. Withholding information will only make things worse. A child's peer group and the group features affect the individuals in the group strongly.

Empowering the Peer Status of your Child through School

Peer groups are important for children. However, the downside is that once they label your child because of their lack of social skills, it can be hard to lose that reputation. Having a reputation, especially one that isn't "cool," can become an obstacle. Negative peer labels are commonly established when the child is in early to middle school, and this reputation does not fade away easily, even though the child develops positive social skills.

Reducing or stopping these negative impacts can be done by establishing a positive working relationship with your child's teachers. Inform them about your child's strengths and desires and the areas with which he struggles. You can also share any approaches that you find helpful in focusing on your child's weakest areas.

A teacher's acceptance, patience, and gentle direction can be an excellent model for the peer group, and influence your child's social status. The teacher plays an important role in finding other ways to draw positivity and positive attention to the child with ADHD.

In the presence of the other children in the school, one way to do this is to give the child special roles and obligations.

Setting Up Accommodations in School and at Home

A good working relationship with your child's teacher enables them to establish ADHD techniques and methods in the classroom that benefit your child in helping him manage his symptoms. Working with a teacher or an adult caregiver, therapist, or coach on effective approaches toward behavior management and social skills is the most practical solution.

Inform your child's teacher about any medication your child takes and whether they need to take it during school hours. Work closely with your child's doctor because you may need to give feedback on your child's responses and symptoms at home and school. Doing so allows the doctor to fine-tune your child's medication.

Chapter 14:
Knowledge About Self-Control

O ne of the things that are normal in children with ADHD is that they act without thinking, which may be a reason they get into trouble. They know the rules, but sometimes they might lose control and forget them. For this reason, you will need to continually adjust rules and restrictions as your child matures.

That is why you should consistently upgrade your child's responsibilities and goals. It tends to be done effectively by going through specific advances that we will discuss in this chapter. Exhibiting terrible behavior doesn't make your child awful. They just struggle with conforming to socially acceptable behavior from time to time.

Connect Behaviors with Consequences

Children experiencing ADHD can't always repress their actions. It tends to be viewed as an issue that they need to manage consistently. Although they generally try, management is difficult and, on occasion, they may carry on without giving thought to the appropriateness of their actions. The simple explanation for this is that they neglect to consider the consequences.

At the point when your child needs to work on this action-consequence association, she should begin by stopping and actively thinking about what could happen if she continued the current course. She should appropriately gauge the outcomes settle on her course of action after considering the situation.

The disconnect between actions and outcomes is an exceptionally normal event among children with ADHD. They don't always think logically and act appropriately when too many stimulating things are happening at once. They can't remember any of the past lessons to help them settle on the right choice. It is the primary justification for why most children with ADHD don't learn from their mistakes. They seem to lack that inner voice that helps us manage our behavior by reminding us that we have done that before, and it didn't turn out well.

So, work with your child to help them foster an association between their actions and results before they find themselves in that situation. You may liken this to a fire drill: we teach children what to do if the building catches fire. In a like manner, if we teach our children what to do in a hypothetical situation—waiting their turn for a piece of cake at a birthday party—they will have a better chance of behaving correctly when they find themselves in that situation.

Go over these scenarios time and again. After that birthday party or social event, review their behavior and point out what they did well and what you need to work on more. All children need positive feedback, and children with ADHD, who often struggle more than others to behave acceptably in public, need more.

At the moment that your child begins misbehaving, redirect her gently. Show her the right action just before she can take the wrong one and ask her to consider the consequences. If you teach your child this lesson in a positive way, then you will have also taught her to be more self-aware.

Setting up an award system helps your child work towards good behavior. Ensuring that she understands right from wrong, and the consequences associated with different behaviors will help encourage her to make good choices. It is your job to be consistent with your child's behavior goals and hand out consequences as soon as possible after poor behavior. Failure to do so will not build the needed connection between behavior and consequence for your child.

Channeling Your Child's Energy to Productive Tasks

Children with ADHD frequently have more energy than they can handle, and it's up to the adults in their lives to help them learn to channel it. Without direction, these children are unable to control their behavior, and is the reason doctors and specialists recommend schedules and activities for children with ADHD. Although you can schedule organized sports and activities for your child to burn excess energy, they will also benefit from free play with attention from their parents. Additionally, there are games that are specifically designed for people with ADHD to help them focus their energy that helps with concentration.

In addition to playing games and scheduling sporting activities, you can create a list of chores for your child to do to keep them occupied. Any child behaves better when they have purposeful tasks that keep them busy, and tasks make them feel as though they are an integral part of the household.

A child with ADHD will find their ability to restrain themselves tested at school where they are required to be still and stay in their seat. You already know that your child has difficulty "hanging tight" for a moment when you need them to do so. They will struggle to behave correctly during class instruction.

One way to help them learn to be still is to offer a choice. Perhaps they want the larger cookie, but to have it, they must sit still for a prescribed period of time. However, they can have the smaller one right now. The point of this is to your child that with patience, they can have more. Waiting helps them control their energy and teaches persistence.

Teaching Your Child to Follow Directions

Children often struggle to follow directions, regardless of their age. Children with ADHD struggle even more, and that's why they are given directions in chunks.

Following directions requires focusing on what is being said so they can remember it, and children with ADHD have difficulty with that. When a child with ADHD is asked to complete a multi-step task, she will struggle because she may only remember three of the four tasks. Therefore, you or a teacher must help her learn to recall the steps. This skill is necessary for success in life.

If you need your child to understand and execute the directions you've given her, you should ensure that you have given them to her in a way she can process them. If you often give directions while doing other things—washing dishes or moving laundry in a noisy laundry room—your child may not understand everything you asked her to do. She will be lost in a universe of her own creation and won't hear a thing you say.

The most effective way to have your child do as you ask is to get her attention. Move close to her and put a hand on her shoulder. This way, you are physically connected, and that will help you stay connected intellectually.

Keep direct eye contact while providing instructions to your child. For example, if you ask her to get ready for school, she does not know what you are asking of her. It's too vague, and she won't be successful. Instead, tell her the steps she needs to take to get ready for school: brush your teeth, change your underwear, put on a clean shirt, put on clean jeans/shorts/skirt, socks, shoes, and so on. Be clear and firm.

If you want to explain something to your child, do that before giving her instructions. If you explain something to your child after giving her the instructions, she will likely forget what you asked her to do.

After you provide the instructions, stay with her to learn how well she listened. This opportunity helps you understand better how to give your child directions so she can successfully execute the task. If you find your child doing what you have asked them to do, praise her immediately so that she feels motivated to continue. However, if you realize she is doing the task completely wrong, she may not have understood you correctly. Instead of being upset with her, talk about the steps she did incorrectly or out of order so she can still be successful.

If she is stubborn and does not comply with the instructions, you can try to implement some 'If' and 'Then' sentences. Doing so will help her understand the potential consequences of her actions. Assuming your child decides to do as you asked, recognize her for being successful. However, if she still refuses to do as you asked, you will have to give her the appropriate consequences for her actions, such as taking away TV time or a favorite toy.

Your approach needs to be consistent and calm, and everyone in the household needs to follow this approach for it to be beneficial to your child. Talk with your partner or spouse to ensure that others are following the same method of giving instructions.

For daily routines, develop a checklist for your child to follow. It will not only help her stay on track but will also help her work independently without constant reminders.

Enhance Your Child's Listening Skills

One of the primary motivations behind why children with ADHD often respond before thinking is that they don't listen appropriately. When your child knows when to talk and listen, she will be more successful in school and have an easier time at home.

Children with ADHD sometimes struggle to tune in to what's happening around them. Although the act of listening seems simple, for your child, it may not be, and you will have to teach her good listening skills. Often your child is waiting for the right opportunity to shout out whatever is on her mind at the moment, and she forgets to listen to the teacher's lesson or the directions you are giving her. But we all know that waiting is a tough job to complete for children with ADHD. You can teach your child a few manners to improve her listening abilities. We should view them.

When you are explaining something to your ADHD child and are unsure whether she is listening, ask her questions so you can be sure she is listening and understanding. Even when you provide instructions clearly, your child might not understand what you've said. Ask her to repeat your directions, which has two purposes. First, you know whether she is listening. Second, you can determine if she understands what you as telling or asking of her.

As you give instructions to your child, clarify every step or stage to ensure she can process your meaning. Use words like first, next, then, and last to help her keep the steps organized in her mind.

Make sure your words are predictable as you talk to your child. Don't use new words that she may or may not understand. Using consistent language gives your child a better chance at understanding you. She needs to know what to expect from you to be calm and secure during the conversation.

Use hand movements as you talk with your child. She will connect the hand movements with the steps or information to better help her remember.

One way to practice listening skills is to watch TV together. Ask your child to explain what just happened. You will be able to understand whether she was listening. Another way to is ask your child what they talked about with a friend on the phone.

Instilling Problem-Solving Skills

Children experiencing ADHD frequently struggle to be calm when they need to tackle everyday issues. Although it may be easily manageable, your child might be overwhelmed and unable to complete the task. The real problem will be lost in all the thoughts swirling around their brains.

There are a few steps that you should encourage your child to use to improve their critical thinking skills.

- Tell your child to ask themselves what the problem is.
- Ask your child to think deeply about each option for a minute and then analyze whether it is a good solution.
- After she is done analyzing, ask your child to select one of the solutions that they think will work.
- Ask your child to try out the chosen option to make sure it will help solve the problem.

You should train your child to tackle their concerns in this way to achieve success, as it is a needed life skill. Additionally, you should teach independence so your child knows she can rely on herself. However, if your child misbehaves correct her, and implement consequences if her actions deserve of them.

If your child struggles to stay organize without help, ask her to write her thoughts down. Then, have a meeting with her to generate new ideas. If her mindset is negative, help her to understand that remaining positive is important to overall success. Show her how to express herself to help control her overall demeanor. In this way, your child will become accustomed to self-moderation when you can't be there to help.

One thing to remind your child: even though they can do things independently, it's okay to ask for help when needed. At whatever point they feel stuck in some place, she can ask for help from anyone she trusts.

Chapter 15:
Choosing Self-Care

There are numerous practical matters to deal with when a child has ADHD. One lesson all children need to know, especially those with ADHD, is that they can care for themselves. However, with children with ADHD, this is something that you will have to teach directly. They won't learn it naturally. However, once they gain independence and are self-reliant in their care, their lives will improve tremendously, as will yours. It is essential to teach your children not to rely on your verbal instructions; they must know what is needed and be able to complete the task.

A common example is teaching your child how to use an alarm clock to wake up in the morning rather than relying on a parent to wake them. This process will be a long one; however, showing your child faith and love will give him the strength to learn.

Whether remembering to use toothpaste when he brushes his teeth or pouring his own juice, your child will gain confidence in everyday activities. He may not be at the same level of independence as others his age, and that's okay. He will learn at his own pace if given the opportunity and support. It is thought that children with ADHD are generally behind other children in their daily activities by almost 30%, and it is most evident in their self-management skills.

There are actions you can take to help your child become an active participant in his self-care.

Concentrating on the Related Advantages

It is common with self-care that many think of spa days and pedicures. However, that is not what self-care is. Self-care is basic personal hygiene, like brushing your teeth, changing your underwear, and putting on socks with your shoes. Your child will benefit in that he can do things the way he likes prefers.

The first step is to help your child understand what he likes and wants. Whenever children with ADHD are not encouraged to engage in self-care or look after themselves, they tend to become more depleted emotionally, depressed, exhausted, and angry. Teaching your child self-care also teaches him that he needs to make himself a priority and reduces the chances that he will be overwhelmed by the process.

As your child grows to a teenager, he might feel that he can look after himself, which may be an unrealistic expectation if you've been doing everything for him at this point. However, if you begin asking questions about self-care early on, the chances are high that your child will be self-sufficient by the teenage years. Take it a step at a time, teaching him the little steps from an early age so that he feels good about himself.

However, there are many cases where children with ADHD struggle with the fear of rejection and abandonment as parents encourage independence and self-care. These fears might stop your child from adapting to a self-sustainable lifestyle. Should your child show these symptoms, you may choose a different approach to teaching self-care. Ask your child, "Do you feel I will love you any less if you take care of yourself?" You will have to make your child realizes that you want him to develop independence. Ensure he knows you are their biggest cheerleader and all that you do is to help him be a successful adult.

To encourage your child to practice self-care, point out the advantages of self-reliance. Give him examples—as he becomes self-reliant, he can go more places and won't have to wait for help to make a snack. The idea is to help your child understand that the long-term goal is not to need anyone's help. Be mindful of your word choice and tone when you talk with your child so that he understands that you are sincere in your wish for him to succeed.

Pay attention to your child's reactions to determine the best path forward. It will help you to keep track of his progress in learning self-care.

Teaching the Importance of Following Through on Commitments

Whenever you try to help your child with ADHD with even the smallest task, you will save time. However, are you helping them become independent? Children with ADHD find it difficult to follow through with anything, be it instructions or commitments, yet there are ways to help your child understand the concept of commitment without triggering and outburst.

Working on Organization Skills

One of the primary challenges faced by parents of a child with ADHD is teaching him to follow through and remember his obligations. The main reason behind this inability is limited organizational skills. Despite that, parents also share some blame in that they unknowingly use ADHD to avoid important tasks and commitments. Just because a child has ADHD doesn't mean he is incapable of being productive. They can wake up to an alarm and work through a day's routine.

One strategy to implement is the use of a planner. Teach your child to use the planner to map out the day. Have him plan his own routine and allow him to write it out himself. For instance, consider that your child has several school assignments due later in the week. Encourage him to write them in the planner so that he remembers that they exist ad on what days they are due. However, documenting information in the planner is only half of the job. Your child must reference the planner throughout the day to ensure he follows through with what needs doing.

Teach your child to break assignments into manageable chunks. Help him understand that he needs to work through the steps one at a time rather than trying to tackle it all at once. In addition to teaching your child how to break down assignments, you also need to teach him time management. After he has broken the assignments into manageable pieces, you might ask him:

- How many different steps are there?
- How long will each one take?
- How long do you have to complete the assignment?
- How many steps must you complete each day to have the assignment ready to submit on time?

These questions help him process the steps so that he can be successful.

In the same way, if any examinations are coming up in your child's school, you will have to teach your child how to prepare a proper study plan to get done with everything on time. Help your child understand the importance of keeping a daily goal in their planner, regardless of how big or small it is. Teach your child strategies for attaining this goal. In this way, steadily and slowly, you can make your child invested in his/her studies.

Introducing Pets to Teach Responsibility

You can use pets to instill a sense of responsibility and routine in your child, because pets bring positivity. Ask your child what pet he wants, be it a rabbit, dog, cat, or another animal. Then, assign your child the task of caring for the pet. He should be responsible for feeding the animal and taking it for walks if they are needed or cleaning the cage or tank. Your child will take care of their pet out of love, and the sense of responsibility boosts his self-esteem.

Dogs and cats are often best as they remind your child if he has forgotten to feed it. Animals come with their ways of making people understand things. Also, gifting a pet to your child will make them feel responsible. At times, a little push is all the motivation needed.

Practicing Color Coding

A great strategy that can help your child with ADHD with their organizational skills is color-coding. The reality is that your child will face some academic challenges. However, that is no reason for him quit. Color coding is a strategy that can help people with ADHD say organized.

A great place to begin is to have your child color code his school subjects in his planner. It will help your child understand what needs his attention with a glance at the planner. For instance, your child assigned math yellow. If he has math homework, he should write the assignment in his planner, then highlight the note or affix a yellow label to it so that he knows it's math.

To further align the idea of color-coding school subjects, have your child use notebooks and folders as well. A yellow notebook, folder, and assignment in the planner for math will help him stay organized.

Another option is to have him wear a yellow bracelet so he knows he has math homework. Using the strategy of the bracelet can help as it serves as a visual reminder of a task. After he turns in his assignment or the teacher checks it, your child can take off the bracelet.

Organizational skills can be made quite strong with the help of color coding. It is a strategy that can be followed by your child easily.

Helping Your Child Create Routines

There is no perfect way to raise a child with ADHD. As with all children, each has unique needs, and you must determine what works best for him. However, one essential thing to remember when parenting a child with ADHD is to create a structured environment on which your child can rely. It includes introducing him to routine.

What Is the Importance of Routine?

"Structure" is often described as a best practice when raising a child with ADHD. So, what is "structure," exactly? Simply put, it is an organized and predictable environment.

To create an effective structure for your child, begin with a schedule that includes everyday routines like brushing their teeth and making the bed.

Because children with ADHD often lack the ability to self-regulate behavior, a structured environment gives them a sense of security. Completing even tough jobs will be relatively easy when there is a fixed routine. They will learn how they can plan time for simple things like brushing their teeth, taking a shower, or even finishing their homework.

One note of caution: your child must understand the expectations, rules, and consequences in that predictable environment for it to be successful in aiding their development as individual adults.

How Can a Routine Be Developed?

There are several ways to help develop a routine for your child.

- **Provide clear instructions.** Children with ADHD need specific information about your expectations. When you ask your child to clean his room, don't simply tell him, "Go clean your room." Instead, be specific. Say, "Make your bed." "Put your shoes in the closet." "Put your dirty clothes in the hamper." "Put the toys in the cupboard and the books on the shelf."
- **Assign tasks he can complete independently.** Only assign tasks you know your child can complete on their own. As they are successful and develop confidence, add to the degree of difficulty. However, if you begin by asking your four-year-old to clean the bathroom, chances are he won't be successful, and the failure will demotivate him. Whereas asking him to put his toys away is an age-appropriate chore that will be easy for him to complete. The only aim is to

develop a proper routine and encourage your child to complete their tasks independently.

- **Don't bundle the tasks together.** Although, as adults, we see that you sweep the floor before you mop it, your child does not. Therefore, if your child needs to complete a larger task, break it down into small steps, just as you do with his homework in his planner. Create sequences of two to five steps. Hang up the list where your child can readily see it. Well-written task lists are better for children with ADHD as they might forget verbal instructions.
- **Don't discount physical activity.** For children with ADHD, physical activities stimulate and help them burn their excess energy. Specialists advise that you schedule time for sports in your child's day.
- **Create a Rules/Rewards system.** A great way to ensure that the method of schedule and routine works for your child is to develop a set of rules that result in rewards. As your child finishes a task, provide the designated prize, whether a treat or five extra minutes with the gaming system.
- **Remember, positive reinforcement.** At times, your child may not seem to be making progress. That happens, and you still need to acknowledge that he is trying to improve. The reward for proper behavior needs to be frequent compared to punishment for doing something bad.
- **Set reasonable expectations.** Change doesn't happen overnight, and it's a foolish parent who believes the changes in their child will be immediate. It takes time for your child to unlearn bad habits and replace them with positive ones. He will try, and if you cheer him on, he will continue to learn.
- **Don't crowd their routine.** Leave some free time for your child to do whatever suits him at that moment. Perhaps it's a game outside or a trip for ice cream if he had a terrific week. Maybe it's just time in his room with a favorite book. Whatever the entertainment, your child needs time without scheduled events.

Helping a Child Deal with Dressing Difficulties

The complete act or task of putting on clothes might be a difficult task for a child with ADHD. However, you can make the task easy by implementing some simple steps. Some children might have sensory issues and struggle with the fabric their clothes are made of, or some might forget the proper sequence they are meant to put on the clothes. The nature of problems will vary from one child to another.

- **Calm your child.** If your child needs to bathe in the morning, dry him with a heavily textured towel. According to some studies, using textured towels has a calming effect on children with ADHD. When your child is calm, dressing will be easier for him. It will also provide your child with tactile stimulation.
- **Sometimes, clothing is not comfortable.** If your child complains about his clothes being itchy, believe him. Whatever the complaint about the fabric, it is real to your child. If he doesn't like boys' sport socks and prefers the smooth inside of dress socks, let him wear dress socks. Choose soft fabrics and ensure tags don't poke.
- **Buy tight-fitted underwear.** Some children with ADHD prefer tight-fitted underwear, which makes them feel secure. If that is the case with your child, try performance underwear designed to fit close to the body. However, ensure that the fabrics are breathable and of high quality, so they do not make the clothing uncomfortable for your child.
- **Keep clothing simple.** Zippers and buttons can confound a young child, and one who might also be impatient may struggle unnecessarily. Choose pants or shorts with elastic waistbands rather than fasteners. Also, give your child lessons in dressing, such as tying his shoelaces and buttoning his shirt.

- **Keep the closet and dresser tidy.** As with everything else, organization is key for your child to gain independence with dressing. Keep his clothing neatly organized in his closet and dresser. Allow him to help determine the pattern—same colors together or same items together. Whatever works for his brain is how you need to keep it.

Chapter 16:
Behavioral Therapy for ADHD

M edication helps an ADHD patient on the neurological level, but therapy is equally important to make day-to-day life easier. Behavioral therapy is a preliminary therapeutic approach that an ADHD patient is exposed to in childhood. As patients age, they graduate into cognitive behavioral therapy (CBT).

How Does Behavioral Therapy Work?

When we talk about going to therapy, we often picture a therapist talking to her patient. But that is not how every type of therapy looks. Behavioral therapy is quite different. Here, the person's emotions are not the primary focus; rather, the focus is on the actions and how the patient can rectify them.

When a child or an adult visits a therapist, the therapist evaluates the problem and then designs a treatment plan to help solve the problem. The idea is to eliminate toxic, negative habits and replace them with positive ones. For children, behavioral therapy also involves their parents.

Many parents of children with ADHD become frustrated and yell at their child when she misbehaves, even though she did not act with intent. So, a major part of behavioral therapy is also about helping parents understand their children and change their behaviors toward their children.

No matter the type of behavioral therapy, it is a system of rewards and consequences. The rewards must motivate the patient and make her work hard to achieve her goals.

Children are taught to understand situations and act accordingly. Additionally, they are taught self-control techniques. Since the main aim is to teach good habits on which the child can fall back, the chosen therapy rewards should reinforce a patient's good behavior.

If you notice that rewards are not helpful, you must take a different approach. That is when the concept of consequences, particularly negative consequences, is implemented. If the patient does not do something as asked, she loses points, TV time, or a treat.

Choose a Therapist

Before learning how to choose a good therapist for your child, you need information about the different therapies that exist. It will be the mental health professional who evaluates and treats your child who will be able to tell you which therapy method would work best. However, you should also be open to trying new methods. Following are four common therapies.

The Main Types of Therapy

Play therapy is used for preschool or elementary school children who have experienced something traumatic or stressful. In this therapy, the therapist will use games, art, and toys to help the child express their feelings while talking to them.

Cognitive behavioral therapy (CBT) is used with children with mood disorders, compulsions, and phobias. Therapists will teach your child techniques to overcome these behavioral issues or perhaps help get to the bottom of her fears to overcome those as well.

The third main type of therapy is talk therapy, which is the most common type of therapy. In these sessions, your child will talk with a therapist, and the therapist will listen. Your child will understand and express her feelings, improve communication skills, develop problem-solving skills, and form stronger, healthier relationships.

The fourth main type of therapy is group therapy. If your child has trouble socializing, group therapy might be a good fit for her. She can learn the skills she needs to socialize with others on their level and overcome her difficulties socializing with other children.

The Main Types of Therapists

There are numerous types of therapies and an equal number of types of therapists who specialize in different fields, so there are of course different therapists to suit your individual needs. Each of these therapists have expertise in different fields because each of them have different types of licenses and specializations. They are grouped here according to specializations.

Licensed professional counselors

Licensed professional counselors (LPC) provide therapy to clients individually or in groups; diagnose and treat emotional, mental, and addictive disorders; and research more effective therapy methods both for clients and for the general advancement of the therapy/counselling profession.

Licensed mental health counselors

Licensed mental health counselors' (LMHC) jobs specifics vary widely because mental illness can affect people across different age groups, locations, and social groups. Therefore, many LMHCs specialize in certain specific areas of expertise.

There are several therapist specializations that fall under this category:

- Psychotherapists
- Grief therapists
- Group therapists
- Cognitive-behavioral therapists
- Trauma therapists
- Child therapists

- Behavior therapists

Licensed Marriage and Family Therapist

Another type of therapist are licensed marriage and family therapists. They are trained and licensed to test, diagnose, and treat emotional, disorder, health issues, behavioral issues, and mental disorders. They also have the expertise to deal with relationship dynamics of the type you will find in marriage, family, and couples.

Often, family and marriage therapy yield better results than just simply individual therapy for the people involved. Usually, it works better when mental health problems are involved such as anorexia, childhood autism, mood disorders, and adult alcoholism, to name a few.

Licensed Clinical Social Worker

The fourth main type of therapist is a licensed clinical social worker (LCSW). An LCSW provides treatment to clients with emotional and mental problems that affect their day-to-day lives. LCSWs work with their clients, listen to their emotional and psychological needs, and provide resources to support their clients.

Licensed clinical social workers can diagnose disorders and issues and treat these disorders and issues of the client—though, in the US, this may differ from state to state.

LCSW provide treatment by offering therapy, providing referrals, and working with other professionals to ensure that the best and most effective treatment plan has been created for their client.

Psychologist

A psychologist is a therapist who holds either a PhD or a PsyD. In the US, psychologists are allowed to prescribe medications in five states:

Louisiana, New Mexico, Illinois, Idaho, and Iowa. However, in Europe, psychologists typically cannot prescribe medication.

Psychiatrist

A is a psychiatrist who holds either a MD or a DO. As a medical doctor, a psychiatrist can prescribe medication.

Now that you know the different types of therapies and therapists, you need to know how to choose the correct one for your child.

Questions for Screening Therapists

1. Ask if they have available slots and are flexible around school hours.
2. Ask if they accept insurance, and if so, what companies. If they do not, as their hourly rate.
3. Ask about their background and training in working with children.
4. Inquire whether they have any cultural competency or training in that area.
5. Ask them what kind of therapeutic methods they use for children and teenagers.
6. Ask how often they meet with parents or guardians.
7. Ask if they will be in contact with your child's teacher or guidance counselor.
8. Inquire how long children typically stay in therapy with them.

Cognitive Behavioral Therapy for Adults

Research results indicates that adults with ADHD can benefit from cognitive behavioral therapy (CBT). The patient is not only happier but is also more productive and has an elevated level of self-esteem.

What is CBT?

Cognitive behavioral therapy is a talking therapy that's done over the short term to change how people think and instill healthy thought patterns. Adults with ADHD have already undergone a lifetime of poor self-esteem, continually missing deadlines, and forgetfulness. This goal-oriented therapy involves psychotherapy concepts and can help the patient change her thoughts about the world, herself, and her future. Negative thoughts are replaced with positive ones. In short, CBT is specialized training for the brain.

CBT's main purpose is to change how the patient perceives the events of her life and how she behaves in particular situations. Ultimately, both have an immense effect on how the patient feels. Whether she is dealing with complicated relationships, stress, or negativity, CBT can help.

Studies have proven the usefulness of CBT for a variety of conditions, including:

- Drug and alcohol use
- Anxiety
- Depression

It has also been noticed that compared to other forms of psychiatric medications, CBT has better results.

CBT is based on these principles:

- Every psychological problem is the result of faulty thought patterns.
- Every psychological problem is the result of learned behavioral patterns.
- Patients can learn better coping methods to help them manage their symptoms.

Simply put, CBT is a goal-oriented treatment method specific to the problem at hand. It addresses the patients' behaviors, thoughts, and challenges they face. CBT is successful as group or one-on-one therapy sessions.

Initially, CBT was used to treat people suffering from mood disorders and then branched out to other conditions. All of us have automatic reactions to situations, but for some, these thoughts are the reason they face problems in their emotional state. CBT addresses these thoughts and helps correct spontaneous interpretations, which are often flawed. These internal dialogs are so ingrained in our minds that they obstruct making the right decision. So, mental distortions will hinder progress whenever you are trying to calculate the risk or do something productive.

Staying on task for an extended period and completing tasks will be easier with CBT because the problematic thought patterns are changed, so behavior patterns change.

How Does CBT Help ADHD Adults?

As you already know, a person's self-regulation skills are affected by ADHD, which, in turn, impacts an adult's executive functioning skills. It is also why adults with ADHD suffer from emotional dysregulation, poor time management skills, inconsistent motivation, disorganization, procrastination, and impulsivity.

It is often seen that adults who have been diagnosed with ADHD have a pessimistic attitude towards life and are overly self-critical. When situations don't go as planned (which is often the case), ADHD patients blame themselves. Worse, these patients project their pessimistic thoughts into their futures. Their logic follows that because they had a bad day, the rest of the week will be terrible.

ADHD patients can't see the illogic nature of their thought processes because they are clouded by their demoralizing beliefs and thoughts. It also hinders their possibility of growth and productivity.

Following are some distorted thinking patterns that adults with ADHD experience. CBT helps in correcting all these patterns.

- **All-or-nothing thinking.** This type of thinking pattern is when a person consistently uses words like ever or never (i.e., absolute words), and it is common regardless of an ADHD diagnosis. When a patient indulges in this type of thinking, she can only think in extremes. This faulty thinking pattern also makes her overlook alternative solutions that might be present. And in the case of an ADHD patient, she only thinks about the negatives. The patient either sees themself as a complete failure or thinks she is a success. If she makes a small mistake in a project, she immediately discredits her efforts to that point and considers herself a failure.
- **Mind reading.** This cognitive distortion is when someone assumes she knows what the person in front of her is thinking. It is dangerous. After all, she may fail to notice what is real because she is caught up in what she *thinks* is real. She relies so heavily on her self-proclaimed ability to read minds that she misreads others' intentions. It leads to sudden bouts of frustration and anxiety. The direct result of mind reading is social anxiety. In the case of ADHD patients, this is even more magnified because ADHD adults already suffer from a certain extent of social anxiety.
- **Overgeneralization.** Overgeneralization is when a person makes broad assumptions about things despite limited experience. Overgeneralization can manifest in several forms but mostly revolves around the fact that once a person notices something negative, she thinks everything will be negative. In short, she allows one singular event to predict every outcome that is to follow. For example, she didn't get the job after an interview. She then thinks she will not get any job for which she interviews because she is not good enough. This thought process brings about a feeling of hopelessness.
- **Fortune-telling.** With this cognitive distortion, the roots are based on anxiety. ADHD patients claim they know the future and that it will be bad. When a patient predicts based on

assumptions, she is fortune-telling. Thus, the real odds are never considered, so she cannot call fortune-telling a true assessment. For example, if her job interview went bad, she will assess it. But as there is no way of knowing for certain she will get the job, and there are hundreds of reasons she may or may not, assuming that she didn't get the position is fortune-telling.

- **Personalization.** This cognitive distortion affects adults with ADHD. In this type of negative thought pattern, the patient blames herself or someone else for everything that went wrong. However, the truth may be that the situation was out of control, and no one was at fault. For example, when a patient does not perform professionally, she blames herself. If only she had put in more effort, there would have been no complications. But things are not like that–ADHD is a problem with symptoms that hamper everyday life.

- **Comparative thinking.** This type of thinking brings inferiority complexes and makes us feel we cannot achieve things. ADHD patients have been commonly found to give in to comparative thinking. Every person on earth has her weaknesses and strengths, and comparisons are not something that you should do.

- **Mental filtering.** This specific faulty thought pattern is found in patients with ADHD and others. When a person has the habit of mental filtering, she filters out all the positives and focuses on the negative. She always finds her glass half empty. Often rooted in loneliness, she is so focused on her dissatisfaction and inadequacies that she misses the fun. The most effective method of overcoming this mental filtering is to reframe negative thoughts.

- **Emotional reasoning.** Another cognitive distortion commonly seen in ADHD patients is emotional reasoning, where she thinks reality is reflected in her negative feelings. Let's say she is tense. Emotional reasoning pushes her to believe that she is in danger. This often leads to exaggerations of insignificant problems.

In CBT sessions, the therapist will help you understand your thoughts, and you will learn to identify the different cognitive distortions. When you widen your perception of a situation, your reactions are less defensive. Through CBT, you will address your fears and insecurities through various activities, such as role-playing. You will have homework assignments to practice what you learned. In time, you will no longer jump to conclusions or fall back on a negative mindset as your default setting.

One common problem among patients with ADHD is procrastination. Keeping track of time is a major issue, but not everyone suffers in the same way. For each patient, the therapist will ask her to describe a recent situation where procrastination got the better of her. After listening to the incident, the patient and therapist will set a specific goal, which may be something as commonplace as grocery shopping.

The patient's relationship to the task is analyzed to help the therapist devise a plan for the patient to follow. The task will be broken down into simple, actionable steps. Each step is then analyzed to determine if there are potential barriers. If there are barriers, they will discuss what steps can be followed to overcome those barriers. Throughout the discussion, the therapist will ask her patient about their thoughts during each step. She will also ask her patient what emotions they feel about finally facing the task that they had been putting off for so long.

Remember, for CBT to be successful, you need a therapist who handles ADHD patients. ADHD specialty clinics are more prevalent, and you can contact these clinics for qualified therapists in your area. Another thing for which you will get help from CBT is comorbid conditions. Hypersensitivity often leads to anxiety, and CBT helps address all the issues and comorbid conditions of ADHD. Every condition is treated with a different approach in the case of CBT.

What is Dialectical Behavior Therapy?

Dialectical behavior therapy (DBT) is like CBT because it also focuses on mitigating the challenges faced by a patient on an emotional and social level. Initially, it was only the patients of borderline personality disorder who were treated with DBT. Now, it is used in numerous situations.

DBT therapy focuses on teaching emotional regulation skills, and in the case of ADHD patients, these skills prove to be fruitful in leading an everyday life.

The Pros and Cons of ADHD Medication

There are several types of medication used to treat ADHD and each has specific uses.

- **Stimulants**

Some methylphenidates (stimulants) include dexmethylphenidate (sold as Focalin); methylphenidate (sold as Ritalin, Concerta, Daytrana, Jornay PM, Metadate, and Quillivant XR); and serdexmethylphenidate and dexmethylphenidate (sold as Azstarys).

- **Non-stimulants**

Nonstimulants typically do not work as well as stimulants. The goal of raising chemical levels is to help your child concentrate, reduce impulsivity, and increased calmness. Nonstimulants are not divided into subgroups.

They are available as atomoxetine (sold as Strattera); clonidine (sold as Kapvay); viloxazine (sold as Qelbree); and guanfacine (sold as Intuniv).

How ADHD Medication May Affect Your Child

Since research has proven that the long-term use of ADHD medication is safe, ADHD medication can be taken for years or a lifetime.

- **Long-Term Effects (Pros)**

There are benefits to long-term usage of ADHD medication. Using large national and insurance databases, scientists are seen that patients with ADHD who take medication have a lower risk of engaging in criminal activity, have lower rates of suicidal behavior, have fewer vehicle accidents, lower risk of traumatic brain injury, and lower rates of substance abuse.

- **Short-Term Effects (Pros)**

Fascinatingly enough, there are many beneficial short-term effects of ADHD medication. It positively influences multiple neuropsychiatric and behavioral factors, such as vehicle accidents, education, injuries, and substance abuse.

- **Long-Term Effects (Cons)**

Some, but not all, children continue their ADHD medical treatment into adulthood. Research identified a correlation between taking ADHD stimulants into adulthood and a slighter stature. However, this has not been confirmed.

- **Short-Term Effects (Cons)**

Reactions in children using ADHD medication vary. Depending on the medication, effects may appear in as little as an hour to a couple of weeks. Typically, the effect of stimulants is seen much faster than the effect of non-stimulants.

It is important to note that, as with all medication, your child will experience some side effects while it is in her body. Like the medicinal effects of medications, the side effects of stimulants differ from the side effects of non-stimulants.

Common side effects of stimulants include weight loss, social withdrawal, sleep problems, and low or no appetite. These include a bad mood or more activity as the meds wear off, a minor delay in growth, and tics (involuntary movements). Very rarely, some patients experience bizarre behaviors, high blood pressure, and higher heart rates.

Common side effects of nonstimulants include stomach pain, drowsiness, nausea, a drop in blood pressure, and tiredness.

Remember that these side effects may only affect your child in the beginning as their body adjusts itself to the medication. If they are nervous, irritable, or seem more dazed than usual, their dosage is likely too high; speak with the prescribing doctor for direction on how to proceed.

The effects of ADHD can be categorized as long-term or short-term, and pros or cons. Ultimately you must and decide whether your child will benefit from ADHD medication. You must be the one who must weigh the pros versus the cons. Keep in mind both the short- and long-term effects and consult your child's mental healthcare professional.

Chapter 17:
Activities for Children with ADHD

I t might feel as if nothing we do is adequate as a parent of a child with ADHD. Your child constantly has extra energy, or whatever they're doing doesn't hold their interest.

It's not that what you're doing isn't sufficient. Different activities and criteria are required of children with ADHD to assist them to remain focused and develop skills. They'll flourish if they're given the proper support.

There are numerous strategies to help your child improve his motor control, emotional regulation, and self-esteem while also enhancing his academic abilities.

Sports for Different Types of ADHD Children

Many psychologists and doctors promote exercise for children to improve their attention spans and self-esteem. It works in adults, but it's especially crucial for children who are constantly evaluating their place in society.

Children with ADHD should engage in activity three or four times a week. Consider enrolling your child in a sport to foster excitement for team or individual play and help develop a routine.

But which activity will have the most significant impact on your child's self-esteem and health? Their ADHD style will determine the ideal sport.

Sports for Children with ADHD and Inattentive Presentation

If your child has an inattentive presentation, he will benefit from a calm sport or fitness activity. That means a team sport's hectic environment, with people on the field at the same time, may be more than he can handle. The noise of the activities may overwhelm him.

Try a sport where one person does one activity at a time or an independent sport where they don't have to pay attention to numerous things at once. Sports like baseball (without sending them in the field) or cross country and track may be suitable for inattentive youngsters.

Sports for Children with a Hyperactive Presentation

Taking full advantage of his workout experience, the child with hyperactivity will struggle with team sports. His restlessness and inability to focus on a single objective for an extended length of time make it difficult for him to operate well with a team in a sporting event's fast-paced and chaotic environment.

Any sport in which children are given one precise aim for a short period (with the fewest potential distractions) will work effectively. Consider the activity's loudness and tempo as well. You need it to be interesting, without a lot of yelling and shouting from the sidelines from coaches or parents. Sports that allow your child work independently, such as martial arts, boxing, swimming, or tennis, are also beneficial.

Before enrolling in any activity, monitor your child in the classroom to ensure that they are comfortable.

Social Groups for Children with ADHD

If your child is young or not interested in sports, don't make him participate in activities he doesn't enjoy or from which he derives no benefit. There are ways to socialize outside that aren't always sports-related!

Consider scouting—Cub Scouts or Boy Scouts. Look for small groups that are highly organized and aren't too noisy. A group like that, along with an activity your child is passionate about, will set him up for success. In addition, the increased sociability will benefit children in other contexts with their classmates.

Art Therapy for Children with ADHD

Art projects, like academic projects, might expose issues with your child's concentration, memory, and decision-making abilities. However, unlike school, the low-stress, low-stakes circumstances around art therapy may increase these functions and improve his emotional well-being and social connections. Many youngsters with ADHD find that visual representations and art are more effective in communicating feelings and thoughts.

Planning time for art in your child's calendar can help him develop critical skills and foster healthy emotional expression. Though the name "art therapy" may conjure up images of seriousness, your child will find it to be a soothing and creative experience.

Steps to a Productive Art Therapy Session in Easy Steps

Focus on your child's effort rather than the outcome throughout the session.

- Remove all visual distractions from the child's workplace. Make the space as clean and neat as possible.
- Use tape or another barrier to outline the area so that your child can stay "within the box" while creating.
- Begin with a light warm-up activity, such as basic coloring, to let off steam or get in the mood to create.
- Select a major art project with clear, easy-to-follow instructions. For increased connection, do it with your child (but not for them!)

Tell your child you like how they carefully followed the directions, stayed concentrated for a long time, and battled past his initial struggles.

Games Along with Art Therapy

If you're looking for home-based activities, you may require more indoor than outside activities. In these cases, you may play various activities with your child to help him relax and burn energy in a healthy way in conjunction with art therapy.

- Scavenger Hunt in the House
- Bubble Print Paintings: Have your child paint a piece of bubble wrap, then press the paper against it to make "bubble print" paintings!
- Twister: an oldie but a goodie!
- Balloon Volleyball
- Hallway Hopscotch
- Structured movement activities
- Dance party

Children with ADHD have a great deal of energy to expend compounded by a problem following orders or cooperating with others, which makes team sports challenging. If this describes your child, one method to assist him in achieving his social and health objectives is to help him access more organized activities such as karate, yoga, or tennis. These planned movement activities allow children to collaborate with others, giving them the benefits of being a part of a team while also offering a fantastic way to burn off energy.

Preschooler Activities

Here is the list of activities for preschooler children with ADHD.

Treasure Quest

Make a list of objects that you hid around the house and offer it to your child. Searching for the objects may assist both the body and the mind stay active. Just make sure the mission is appropriate for your child's age and ability. Here are some age-appropriate suggestions.

Preschoolers can try this variation: Use pictures to show your youngster what they should look for.

Grade-schoolers can try this variation: Make a list of items to look for alongside your child, but keep some open-ended, like "something to draw with."

Tweens' variation: As a hint, use riddles. Find anything that becomes wetter as it dries, for example. (A towel)

Bubble Wrap Activity

Bubble wrap may be used to inspire a variety of activities. Allow your toddler to stroll along the "runway" made of bubble wrap. Make a hopscotch pattern out of bubble wrap squares. Alternatively, put letters on the bubbles using permanent markers and watch how soon your youngster can "pop" the alphabet. You could even let the children color the bubble wrap before putting paper on top of it. They'll have magnificent "bubble print" artwork when the bubbles explode.

Balloon Volleyball

It doesn't get much easier than this. Blow up a balloon and mark the "net" on the ground with a piece of tape. Balloon volleyball is a fun activity for two or more children, but one child may also play it. If no one else is available, have your youngster switch sides by sprinting back and forth across the line, trying to strike the balloon before it hits the ground.

Tweens' variation: If you have more than one child participating, you may increase the number of balloons to keep the game trickier.

Hopscotch in the Hallway

For this dynamic game, all you need is open floor space, a coin to put in the squares, and painter's tape.

Make a hopscotch pattern using the tape. Make tape numbers in each box. You may even build the pattern with triangles, circles, or stars rather than the standard boxes if you're both feeling creative. Then be ready to jump!

Biking

A study was conducted in 2012 to quantify the impacts of riding a bike five days a week. Two groups of youngsters in middle school who were either confirmed with ADHD or showed indications of the disorder were encouraged to ride bikes.

Bicycling, they discovered, improves attention, and reduces impulsivity, improves information processing, improves a child's mood, and allows children to comprehend their feelings better. After just one ride, cognitive performance improved and waist circumference and BMI decrease.

It is why integrating a short bike ride into your children's daily routine might help your youngster focus and be happier.

Music

Singing is not only a fun way to spend time; it also offers additional advantages. Singing aids in developing language in young children and can enhance focus and social skills in people of all ages.

Learning to play a musical instrument, such as the drums, recorder, or piano, can boost confidence, enhance attention, and reduce stress.

According to some studies, music can reduce impulsivity and even increase mathematical skills in youngsters with ADHD.

Playing music and having a dance party is a terrific unplanned approach to assist your child in burning off energy while you realize they are becoming restless. It is a fantastic technique to let children get their wobbles out while also helping to reset everyone's attitude.

Drama

Your child will be able to put oneself in somebody else's shoes via acting and role play. As he leaves his shyness behind and gets into character, learning lines and preparing to walk on stage will educate them on self-discipline. Drama is a great way to assist children in enhancing their social skills while also improving their focus, understanding, and confidence.

Storytelling

Sharing a tale with your child is a wonderful way of connecting with them and helping them view the world in new ways. Children with ADHD sometimes overlook character motives but reading together and discussing the various characters' behavioral intentions might help him better understand others.

Masking Tape Activity

With little more than a roll of masking tape, you can create many entertaining activities. Create a hurdle course of straight and zigzag lines for your child to complete by crawling, leaping, walking backward, and holding something heavy in an indoor game of hopscotch or tic-tac-toe. When you're done, ask him to remove all the tape to help him calm down.

Board Balancing

A basic balancing board is an excellent alternative to explore if you need activities that don't involve a lot of preparation or clean-up.

Balance boards help in your child's development of gross motor skills and balancing abilities. It also gives him the physical release that children with ADHD frequently require.

Egg Races

Consider setting up some fun birthday party activities, such as egg races, if you're trapped at home on a rough weather day and require something to keep the children occupied.

Begin with a basic sprint across the living room and gradually increase the game's difficulty by placing pillows and blankets on the floor. You may even have your child alternate among their right and left hands to provide an extra twist to the game and keep it going!

Balloons

Blow up a few balloons and then let your youngster throw them around the room or go all out and set up an indoor balloon volleyball game. You may also get some rackets and host an indoor balloon tennis game. The options are truly limitless!

Jumping Rope

Jumping rope is an excellent activity for children with ADHD if you have a large enough space with high enough ceilings. It's portable, enjoyable, helps with coordination, and burns a lot of calories!

Hula Hooping

Hula hooping is a fun, affordable core workout that the whole family will enjoy. Challenge one another to find who can maintain their hula hoop in action the longest, and if you have a lot of hula hoops, you can make obstacle courses out of them.

Trampoline or Workout Ball Bouncing

No list of ADHD activities would be complete without a trampoline or exercise ball! Jumping certainly helps children burn off a lot of energy, and each of these items provides a low-cost method for children to get their wiggles out while confined indoors. You may keep it basic by having your youngster jump on an exercise ball and bounce on an indoor trampoline.

To keep things interesting, have your child alternate between the two activities for a count of ten, or have them roll and kick the ball all over the floor, or have them lie on their belly on top of the ball and see how long they can stay balanced without holding onto anything.

Obstacle Courses

Setting up many gross motor exercises into an obstacle course may be a lot of fun while children are confined indoors. Cushions, masking tape, an exercise ball, hula hoops, a jumping rope, indoor tunnels, or any props you have laying around the house may be used in various ways.

Getting Wet in Puddles

Rain doesn't seem to bother children as much as it does adults, so putting on a raincoat as well as some rain boots and allowing your child to get sloppy and muddy may be what they need to burn off some energy on a rough weather day.

Battle of the Water Balloons

A water balloon fight is extremely popular if you're searching for activities for children with ADHD, and it also serves as a fun method for youngsters to hone their throwing abilities!

Head, Shoulders, Knees, and Toes

You may make it more difficult by increasing the song's tempo or allocating various body parts, such as head for nose, shoulders for chest, knees for hips, and toes for heels. You may also make the game a mental teaser by playing it backward.

First Year

We compile a list of suggestions for allowing pupils to fidget quietly. Here are a few of our favorites:

Squeeze the Balls

Many items can be squished discreetly, including stress balls, squishy balls, Koosh balls, and hand exercisers. Teacher tip: Ensure pupils put them beneath their desks, so they don't bother others.

Silly Putty

Students can also use Playdoh, silly putty, or Sticky Tack to keep their hands engaged.

Chewable Necklace

Gum chewing can help some ADHD children stay focused.

Doodling

Many children, not just those with ADHD, benefit from doodling. Some benefit from doodling during story time or throughout a lesson.

Music in Background

Some children may benefit from a fan in the room's rear to help them concentrate.

Leg Bands for Chairs

Students can push or pull against a big rubber band (or yoga band) tied around two front legs of the chair.

Disk Seat

These attach to a chair and allow children to swing in their seats rather than the entire chair, which is less harmful. Cushions also work.

Standing Desk

Standing desks are an excellent idea all children, not just fidgeters. Treadmill desks are also an option if your budget allows it.

Desks with Moveable Footrest

Foot tapping may be made quieter with the aid of a built-in footrest.

Room to move around in the classroom

Allow students to stand up, stretch, dance, jog, or swirl in a designated space at the side or rear of the room.

Flexible Workspace

Students don't have to finish their homework at their desks; they can work on the windowsill, switch desks, or sit on the floor. Various learning stations can assist students of all sorts.

Chapter 18:
ADHD Management

T here are numerous ways to manage your child's ADHD, from behavior training to diet.

Anthropometrics

"Anthropometrics" means body measurements, which include height, weight, head circumference, mid-arm circumference, and other measurements. A person's anthropometric measurements are then compared against reference standards. Children are compared using standardized growth charts; several are available, with the most used ones published by the Centers for Disease Control and Prevention (CDC). These growth charts use the measurements of thousands of children in the United States of a given age and gender and establish average percentiles.

Growth charts are not the only way that a child should be monitored for nutritional status and health, but they are helpful for forming an overall understanding of their health and nutrition status. Weight status as indicated by BMI for adults is explained in the table. Comparison of their BMI against the average standard using the CDC growth charts can explain the weight status of a child. He is considered overweight if the BMI for age is greater than the 85th but less than the 95th percentile, and obese if greater than the 95th percentile BMI/age. However, serial measurements plotted over time to monitor the trend of the growth is more important than the actual point on the chart. Access the CDC website for growth plotting charts if needed.

From a calorie consumption standpoint, children ADHD consume more sugar sweetened beverages (SSBs) than others, accounting for almost half of daily fluid intake. They don't drink much water or non-caloric beverages.

Height

Some children with ADHD take medication to help minimize their symptoms. However, one of the side effects of the medication is slower growth. There is some belief that a child will grow more once they discontinue the use of medication.

This fact also promotes the idea that the healthy choice should be the default choice for food establishments, especially in hospital cafeterias and other healthcare settings.

An example of a "default choice" for healthy eating is when a hospital cafeteria uses a whole grain bun for a grill item unless the customer specifically asks for a white bun, and all pre-made deli sandwiches presented for sale are on whole grain, high fiber breads.

Weight Loss

Once children with ADHD take stimulant medications like methylphenidate, they are then more at risk of being underweight than overweight or obese.

Stimulant medications are well-known for causing decreased appetite and weight loss. This may be due to nausea or that the medications stimulate neurotransmitter activity in the brain leading to a slow-burn type of "flight or fight" response. This chemical response from the neurotransmitters can lead to decreased appetite.

Sometimes children adjust to the new medications and regain their appetite, but others don't.

Getting Started with Your Action Plan

By the time your child receives a positive ADHD diagnosis, the diagnosis is made with a ratio of 6 to 6, which stands for six inappropriate and disruptive symptoms during the prior six months in the categories of both Attention Deficit and Hyperactivity and/or Impulse control.

Once you have the diagnosis, your starting point is to look at the list of the 6 to 6 pertaining to your child and discover some alternate ways to help them deal with issues that arise at home and school other than the ways in which they did so, which were inappropriate and disruptive.

Coping with Your Child's ADHD

Some of the challenges you may find yourself facing will include getting your child who has ADHD to perform various tasks, including:

- Following directions and instructions
- Controlling impulses that lead to behave with poor judgment
- Starting and finishing schoolwork
- Keeping their rooms clean
- Listening
- Focusing
- Conforming with authority

You will not only need to act as a parent to them but often an advocate for them to try to ensure that they are treated fairly in a world that can be ignorant and even harsh regarding any disability.

Have a Contact Plan in Place

Be clear about the best ways to reach you during school hours, such as at your office or cell phone. Also, be clear about when you should be contacted, such as if your child has injured themself or another child, had a major tantrum, and so forth.

You can use the information to gather what works most effectively with your child in given situations and what does not. For example, "If my child has a major tantrum, try X, then Y. If neither works, call me to come to pick him up from school. If you do not reach me, please call my mother, Mrs. Smith, at [telephone number]."

"If my child runs away from you in the playground, tell her to freeze, take a time out, and a deep breath. If she keeps running, turn it into a game: 'You win that game, Mary!' If she child runs and you have no way to catch her, roll a ball and ask her to bring it back to you. If they keep running, ensure they do not leave the playground or school premises and always keep an eye on them until they run out of steam.

No doubt, you will be able to create customized strategies that will work with your child and meet your preferences as parents.

In the same way that you would train a puppy to keep it safe, train your child to stop what they are doing and come when called, to not play when crossing the street or standing on the pavement near the street. Practicing this repeatedly every day can help a great deal with coping with your child's impulsiveness and hyperactivity.

It will also help the school staff deal with the unexpected and not have to call you to take your child out of school for every incident. Prepare for the worst, but hope for the best, and at least no one will be caught off guard by anything your child might do.

Advocating for a Child with ADHD

Some of the challenges facing you as a parent of a child with ADHD cause frustrations, such as:

- The sometimes-inflexible school system
- The medical profession
- Feeling that you are not being heard regarding your concerns for your child
- In the conviction that your child might not be getting fair treatment in all respects
- Your child's lack of control
- Society's lack of understanding of ADHD

You will also deal with several personal issues regarding your own health:

- Exhaustion (particularly if your child has any sort of sleep disorder due to their ADHD)
- Finding support from people who understand what you are going through
- Feeling you have enough knowledge to be able to cope
- Feeling guilty over having a child with a disability
- Feeling guilty over sometimes being fed up or disappointed with your own child

Challenges of ADHD and Twenty-First Century Life

As a twenty-first-century parent, you have probably been proactive for your child. You have read up on ADHD and feel dismayed at all the factors affecting diagnosis. You might even be feeling more confused and overwhelmed than ever before.

Researchers are only just beginning to understand that the pressures of our fast-paced society and the early multi-tasking forced on our children from technology and how they may have a detrimental effect on focus and concentration.

Television

One recent study has shown that television can be a real distraction for young children. They became fixated on the screen even when the news was turned on in the background, something that they could not possibly understand.

Some contend that certain shows cause extreme excitability in children, who remain wound up long after the show has ended. Children should avoid watching television before going to school.

If you work outside the home, as most mothers do, you may carry an extra burden of guilt or worry about not being there enough for your child's special needs.

A lot of parents have allowed television and videos to become a free babysitter for children, but new studies have shown that they do not learn as much from television as had been assumed.

Schooling

One of the main problems with children with ADHD is that they have trouble interacting in an appropriate manner with others. You might have great help from teachers and healthcare professionals, while you have been frustrated with others while working to understand what is troubling your child.

Some teachers willingly work with parents and children to develop a sensible action plan, while others just want to lay down the law and stick to the rules regardless of what issues your child may have.

If you have experienced the latter type of educator as opposed to the former, you might even have reached the point at which you have seriously considered taking your child out of a school system that doesn't understand them or ADHD.

At the same time, this course of action can stir up a whole set of issues, namely the effect on your child's social development if you choose to homeschool, and how you can ever manage all the effort and education that will be required if you do decide to go this route.

Medical Care

If you are new to ADHD, you will need to learn all you can about the condition, but you will need to be sure that you are looking at reliable sources based on solid facts, not current popular theories thrown up on websites that have no basis except mere opinion.

You will also want to avoid any sensationalist media websites as well (have you noticed that suddenly every new study on any health topic has suddenly become a headline on the six o'clock news?).

Despite the advances of modern-day medical understanding, human nature is still affected by cultural, religious, and historical bias (though hopefully, those sorts of attitudes are far less common than they were even a decade ago).

The fact is that those who are the most vocal about ADHD not existing have most likely never experienced the unique challenges of being a person with ADHD or parenting a child with ADHD.

Conclusion

Parenting a child with ADHD can be a difficult, stressful process. Knowing what to expect, which strategies might help your child's behavior and taking advantage of treatment options are important aspects of parenting with ADHD.

Parenting with ADHD can be a challenging experience for families, but it does not have to be. Although learning how to parent a child with ADHD successfully takes time, it is possible. Research has shown that children who receive positive parental attention and participate in activities with their parents are less likely to develop psychological or behavioral problems, including ADHD.

Because ADHD is a chronic disorder that requires long-term management, parents must understand their children's needs and know how to appropriately manage their children's behaviors to develop a relationship with their children that enables them to reach their full potential.

Parenting a child with ADHD involves vital communication tasks, such as talking through issues, problem-solving, and planning activities. Because parents are the main caretakers of a child, their lives are affected more than anyone else's by their child's ADHD. So, to take a break from the stresses of parenting, they need to learn how to manage stress and relax.

Understanding your child's disorder and the behaviors it may produce is the first step to developing effective parenting strategies. Children with ADHD have normal intelligence and abilities but may have difficulty in certain areas, such as organization, time management, and waiting for their turn. These difficulties can be minimized by teaching them how to complete tasks and waiting their turn while maintaining self-control.

These strategies can help parents understand their child's issues. For example, children with ADHD may have trouble listening to instructions or following directions from others. These communication problems are more evident when the child feels frustrated or overstimulated. Because of this, parents must learn to recognize the problems and teach their children how to overcome them by using positive reinforcement methods such as praise for good behavior and consequences for poor ones. Other helpful strategies include limiting distractions, listening and understanding, speaking calmly, developing trust, and positively giving instructions.

Because children with ADHD may have difficulty focusing on a task or activity they wish to avoid, parents must be careful not to frustrate their children by forcing them to do something they don't want to do. Instead, parents must teach their children to self-regulate and focus on the task.

Taking advantage of some of the symptoms of ADHD, like hyperactivity, can be a positive experience for both parents and children. Parents can teach their children about physical fitness, improve their gross motor skills, and help them learn social skills through appropriate activities like biking, running, skateboarding, playing catch, or swimming. They can also teach their child to use physical activity as a reward when they complete all their schoolwork or behave well during the day.

Children with ADHD may have problems with self-regulation, and their behavior may seem unpredictable because they have difficulty focusing on what is most important at any moment. Many people may not understand why a child with ADHD becomes hyperactive, but parents can help their children by explaining why they have these problems and teaching them about the importance of setting limits.

Maintaining positive relationships with relatives and friends is important for any family member. Many ADHD children are shy because they are self-conscious of their condition or want to improve it. They may feel that they cannot live up to certain expectations set by peers or adults. Teaching your child to be self-confident and explaining that they have valuable skills can improve their social skills and make them feel better about themselves.

Working on your attitude as a parent can help you handle any possible conflicts. If you are constantly frustrated or angry, which can be a symptom of ADHD, you may act out in a parental way, but your child will learn to have negative attitudes about life and relationships. Positive attitudes about yourself and others help your child succeed and build relationships with others.

Increase your communication with your child by setting open-ended goals, encouraging them to express themselves in positive ways, and praising your child for their accomplishments. Providing clear instructions and giving demonstrations can help children follow those instructions. Talking about the next steps in a relationship helps the child feel like they are part of the overall process. If they don't feel they are being heard, they may feel you are manipulating them.

Developing strategies with children with ADHD means planning a consistent daily schedule to incorporate activities that allow them to feel successful and calm. Children with ADHD need extra structure and rules because they may view life as chaotic and unpredictable. Consistency, stability, and high behavioral standards help children with ADHD respond more positively to their emotions.

Parents can work on strategies for managing their child's ADHD by getting support from other parents in similar situations and asking their pediatrician about treatment options for ADHD. By understanding the disorder and developing effective strategies, you can make the best of your family situation and help your child succeed.

Different family members may deal with the stress of ADHD in different ways. Parents must consider how their children express themselves when developing strategies for their children. Some children may feel embarrassed or isolated because of their disorder and not ask for attention or help at home. Others may feel rebellious, angry, or depressed. Parents should figure out what their child needs and how they can help them through the day. Many older children with ADHD may not mention the disorder to their parents. They may feel disabled and undeserving of help, so they avoid telling anyone about their weaknesses and problems. Parents may come to think that there is nothing wrong as their child is doing well enough in school.

Communication anxiety can be a problem for children with ADHD because of difficulties understanding what others are talking about and expressing themselves clearly, verbally, or non-verbally.

Parents play a key role in their children's lives by providing challenging experiences and learning opportunities that give their children with ADHD the skills they need to live successfully with this disorder.

Be their friend, not their parent. Their ADHD may cause them to act out, making them difficult or unapproachable. Don't be a parent in your own home. Just take care of their basic needs, like food and shelter, and give them space to be themselves in the house. Please don't overdo it by meeting their emotional needs. They will not let you do more than that; they need some space to be alone with their thoughts. They may not want or feel comfortable with what you are doing for them as a parent.

Be a parent in the real world. You will have to perform your parenting duties outside the home and be a different person: friendly to them, giving them advice, or telling them what to do. Please don't be mean or harsh about it when you do this. Inform your children that you are concerned about their problems at school or with a friend and that you will assist them in determining what they can do to resolve the situation. If they say something rude or disrespectful, look away from them as if they were invisible. You'll feel less like a parent, and they'll feel more like an outcast the more you ignore them.

Do not abandon your child if they do not respond positively to your encouragement or have a problem with you. They may need more support from an outside source to help them improve at home. Meet with the teacher or counselor who can help your child with his difficulties and set up some behaviors that will lead to success in school.

Parents of children with ADHD often feel frustrated and confused about their roles in helping their children. They may feel overwhelmed by the level of responsibility for teaching their children to live successfully with this disorder. Parents need to be strong and consistent if they will help their children learn how to handle the disorder. They must remain calm, even when a child behaves badly, so that the child can learn from their mistakes.

Author's Note

Dear reader,

I hope you enjoyed my book.

Please don't forget to toss up a quick review on amazon, I will personally read it! Positive or negative, I'm grateful for all feedback.

Reviews are so helpful for self-published authors and your feedback can make such a difference for my book!

Thanks very much for your time, and I look forward to hearing from you soon.

Sincerely,

Amber

Made in United States
Troutdale, OR
02/23/2024